SEARCH

AND

RESCUE

— ROCKY MOUNTAINS —

KENT DANNEN

LYONS
PRESS

Guilford, Connecticut

An imprint of The Rowman & Littlefield Publishing Group, Inc.
4501 Forbes Blvd., Ste. 200
Lanham, MD 20706
www.rowman.com

Distributed by NATIONAL BOOK NETWORK

Front cover: The Rocky Mountains extend below
14,264-foot Mount Evans reached via 14-mile Colorado
Highway 5; the highest paved road in North America.
Back cover: A National Park Service rescue team uses
a litter to extract a fallen hiker from near Adams Falls
in Colorado's Rocky Mountain National Park.

British Library Cataloguing in Publication Information available
Library of Congress Cataloging-in-Publication Data available

ISBN 978-1-4930-3727-8 (paperback)
ISBN 978-1-4930-3726-1 (e-book)

∞™ The paper used in this publication meets the minimum requirements
of American National Standard for Information Sciences—Permanence
of Paper for Printed Library Materials, ANSI/NISO Z39.48-1992.

Printed in the United States of America

To the very many members of search and rescue teams who expend their time, their labor, their wealth, their health, and even their peace so that people they usually do not know may live

CONTENTS

INTRODUCTION

A member of Grand Teton National Park's elite Jenny Lake Climbing Rangers recounted how, when he first came to the Tetons, he made all the mistakes that, when now committed by others, send him on search and rescue missions. Although I have limped out of the Rocky Mountain wilds, I have not required extraction by a search and rescue team. However, three times I have come close.

In my teenage years, I was hiking with teen companions above Lawn Lake in Colorado's Rocky Mountain National Park. We decided it would be fun to throw ourselves in uncontrolled slides down a snowbank. It all was predictably goofy until my head brushed a rock at the base of the bank. As I whizzed by, I felt my short hair brush a stone. After a unison gasp of horror, all of us mindless teens, relieved that I was unharmed, instantly became sober adults. We hiked rather somberly back down the trail.

About ten years later, I spotted a mountain goat on cliffs above a Canadian wilderness lodge. Then not as accustomed to goats as I later became, I laid down my ice axe and grabbed a tripod to steady my hoped-for photos when climbing after the goat.

Attempting a close approach, I encountered a narrow gully filled with snow. Assuming I could kick steps in the snow, I ventured across. The apparent snow actually was more like hard ice. I slipped at the first step and slid rapidly toward the end of the gully, which had been sliced away by glaciers thousands of years before my eager carelessness. Consequently, the end of the gully was a cliff over which I was about to shoot into a fall of hundreds of feet to rocks.

The feet of my tripod were pointed, but only to maybe 5 percent of the length of the pick on my ice axe that I had abandoned below. They certainly could not stop my slide, but I could use the points to guide the slide's direction.

One rock protruded above the ice between me and the cliff. Guiding with the tripod feet, I slammed into that rock, padded by the contents of my pack. I crawled unharmed onto the rock, which was scarcely large enough for both my booted feet. It was an easy jump to dry, non-slick rock on the edge of the gully. In subsequent years, informed by experience, I made much better mountain goat photos. The tripod, however, was thereafter unsuitably unsteady.

The third near miss was a lightning strike that sent sparks against hikers on either side of where I had been standing a few seconds previously. I was among others thrown to the ground in the boom. No one was hurt. We all, though, were significantly terrified. Gasping, we ran at more than 11,500 feet above sea level to escape the storm. About a mile away, another visitor to Rocky Mountain National Park was killed. The sound of sirens added vigor to our legs but no oxygen to our lungs.

Like all other wilderness travelers, I do not expect ever to need the services of a search and rescue team. But I certainly am glad they stand ready, just in case.

———

Humans have needed on occasion to organize themselves to search for and rescue their fellow humans for as long as there have been humans. Even before humans, there were Neanderthals who showed the social concerns and compassion found in the humans who came later. Such traits turn up in archeological sites where these prehumans (or oldest of humans) treated their neighbors' injuries and buried them ritually with flowers. It seems reasonable that the hunter-gatherers who carried out such activities of mutual concern also would set out to search for and rescue missing friends they held in such regard.

Neanderthals died out around thirty thousand years ago, although some modern humans stroll across the landscape carrying a small percentage of Neanderthal genes in their present-day code. Could that shared 2 percent contribute to a search and rescue gene combination?

The first written record of search and rescue is a much more recent four thousand years old, when Abram (later renamed Abraham) gathered men to search for and rescue his nephew Lot. Lot had become a more-or-less collateral captive during a war among kings of various city-states in today's Israel. Genesis 14:14 relates that when an escapee from the battle in which Lot and all his property were taken reported the capture to Abram, the patriarch assembled his force of 318 trained men, which set out to search for and rescue his nephew. When they located Lot's captors at night, Abram divided his force to attack from different sides and rescued Lot with all his property as well as other captives.

And so search and rescue proceeded through the millennia. Military search and rescue was conspicuous and readily reported. But in America, protected (so far) from foreign invasion by its Atlantic and Pacific moats, military searches have been supplemented by search and rescue teams responding more often to natural hazards. Both civilian and military seekers were searching and rescuing victims of nature's whims.

The military led the way in non-conflict search and rescue in 1886, when Private John Coyle was patrolling on foot during the US Army's

Castle Geyser is prominent in Yellowstone's Upper Geyser Basin.

thirty-year stint as guardian of Yellowstone, America's first national park. On August 8 near Castle Geyser in the Upper Geyser Basin, Coyle heard a woman screaming. He followed the screams to a problem still faced by Yellowstone administrators today: visitor lack of caution around geysers and other thermal features uniquely expelling boiling water.

The woman had climbed to the rim of Castle Geyser's cone to look at the interior, and a change in wind shrouded her in steam. Likely in pain and certainly confused, she started screaming.

It was an appropriate response. She was blinded by steam and unable to climb down, not even knowing in which direction lay the deadly throat of the geyser and in which lay the descent to safety. Her footing was slippery on the cone formed by hot water flowing through the gray volcanic rock saturated with slick silica, a lightweight white mineral deposited by geysers and other hot springs.

Coyle's search soon led him to Castle Geyser. He managed to quickly climb the slippery cone, wrap his blue uniform coat around the woman, and lead her off the geyser. On the way, the geyser's steam seriously burned Coyle's face. The United States Life-Saving Service awarded John Coyle a silver medal for his painful heroism. He was the first rescuer to be honored for his valor in a national park.

This book's stories of search and rescue recount various events according to what unfortunate occurrence forced not only military response, but also civilian search and rescue. Most of the stories tell of searches for the lost or for those injured by falls, lightning, wildlife, or other natural hazards in the Rocky Mountains from the Canadian border to the range's southern end in northern New Mexico. Hopefully, this grouping by hazards will be not only the most interesting arrangement for reading, but also the most instructive to avoid natural dangers and reduce the need for search and rescue.

Search and rescue in the Rocky Mountains today is a technical specialty in which professionals hired by government agencies often have rock-climbing training and experience. These pros work not only for the National Park Service but also for non-federal agencies, primarily sheriff's departments. All the professionals also carry out standard law enforcement duties when not engaged in search and rescue.

Providing the bulk of search and rescue effort, rescue groups of unpaid volunteers work with the professional search and rescue teams. The volunteers are usually trained and certified by organizations such as the Mountain Rescue Association. The skills and service of the volunteers equal those of the professionals.

The search and rescue happenings described in these stories are more interesting than most such operations, which tend to be tedious, short, and successful. The goal stated by nearly all the volunteer groups is "that people might live," and search and rescue teams normally succeed in achieving that goal. They serve and undertake extensive training and practice because of goodwill rather than desire for glory and excitement. Times of excitement sometimes, though, do occur. This book examines some of the abnormal, exciting times.

However, the incidents related by these stories were not chosen primarily for their adventure value. Even climbing a cliff protected by a rope while lightning walks about holds interest for only a few such ascents. Rather, these stories illustrate the variety of search and rescue experiences, experiences which both enliven and complicate search and rescue. The war stories, hopefully, are confined to the Rockies' frontier past. Although the wars are over, the fight against bad luck with natural disaster, carelessness, ignorance, and sometimes arrogance goes on in many forms. So search and rescue has been for millennia and likely will be for as long as people respond to the lure of the Rocky Mountains.

WAR

New Mexico's First Governor Killed

O n the evening of January 17, 1847, while visiting a neighbor's house, Charles Bent opened the door to frantic knocking, and two arrows fired by Native Americans from the Taos Pueblo embedded themselves in his head. Nonetheless, he managed to shut the door.

Bent's family dug through the adobe brick of the house to escape to their own residence. There the Pueblos found him, scalped him alive, and finished the job the arrows had begun.

That the arrows failed to immediately kill Bent, the newly appointed civilian governor of New Mexico, indicated that the Pueblos had reason to be angry with the trader. Bent's trading company had been supplying rifles to tribes of horse nomads such as the Cheyenne and Arapaho to the north. Bent and his associates assumed the nomads would use the firearms to kill bison for their marketable hides. The nomads did kill bison for hides traded at Bent's Colorado stores, but they also used the rifles to kill Native farmers, such as the Pueblos at Taos.

Had rifle balls rather than arrows hit Bent in the head, he would have died at once. Instead, his death was prolonged and painful and followed by the dragging of his mangled corpse through the streets of Taos.

Actually, Bent was a casualty of the Mexican-American War begun in May 1846 over a distant boundary dispute in Texas. American General Stephen Watts Kearny carried out a northern war effort by invading New Mexico, capturing it without opposition and marching on to capture California. This seemed like a huge success. Kearny left in New Mexico a relatively small detachment under Colonel Sterling Price to keep order,

Wheeler Peak at the southern end of the Rockies, the highest peak in New Mexico (13,167 feet), rises above Taos Pueblo.

and appointed Charles Bent civilian governor because of his residence and major business connections in New Mexico.

The Mexicans in New Mexico believed that they had not surrendered but had merely made a tactical withdrawal to Chihuahua, where they expected destruction of American invaders followed by a Mexican advance north to recapture New Mexico. However, the outnumbered Americans soundly defeated the Mexicans in Chihuahua and thereby prevented the recapture.

Some Mexicans in New Mexico therefore plotted by themselves to kick out the Americans. Although Mexicans had benefitted from trade with Bent and others along the Santa Fe Trail, elite Mexicans feared (reasonably) that their large land grants would be lost under American governance.

Moreover, they deemed Bent and other Americans to be arrogant. After all, Bent had become rich and a secret partner with some Mexicans in a land grant. He had married into a very prominent Mexican family in Taos, but he was rich, so they thought he must have been arrogant.

After killing Bent and all the other new American officials or associates they could find (fifteen in total, some under great torture), Mexicans and Taos Pueblos united to attack the main center of American government in Santa Fe. The Mexicans had convinced the Pueblos that Americans would prevent the Pueblos from using the land included in Mexican grants for traditional subsistence.

Meanwhile, a trading party led by younger brother William Bent was headed south with more merchandise for New Mexico stores. Word of his brother's death reached William when his traders (who had not yet traveled out of Colorado) could still see Pikes Peak to the north. They pushed over Raton Pass with great fear about what had happened to their New Mexico families in Taos and Santa Fe.

By the time the traders reached Taos, Colonel Price had already led his detachment north from Santa Fe to rescue the American families in Taos. Price's rescuers ran into the Mexican/Pueblo force headed south. The bloody result was severe defeat for the Mexicans and Pueblos followed by a similar bloody defeat in another skirmish. Price then roared into Taos and battered his way into the massive mission church where the surviving Mexican and Pueblo fighters had taken refuge. The leaders of the revolt who had not been killed were captured. Six were put on trial after the traders from Colorado arrived.

Although much relieved that their families were rescued and under Price's protection, the traders (except presumably William Bent) sympathized with the Mexicans and Pueblos. Their relief and sympathy had no effect: All six leaders of the revolt who had survived Price's rescue were hanged. The traders, who had the only available ropes, lubricated the ropes with soap to make the hangman's knots slide more freely to shorten the strangulations. They then quarreled about whether to cut the valuable ropes from the corpses. Revolt from American control never again occurred in New Mexico.

War against Mexico had been opposed by many Americans (for instance, Abraham Lincoln and Henry David Thoreau) because it was seen (correctly) as a Southern attempt to expand the number of slaveholding states. Thereby, slavery would be protected by maintaining the balance of power in the US Senate.

The implication of the war changed drastically, however, when ten days before its end with the Treaty of Guadalupe-Hidalgo, gold came to light in recently American-captured California. This huge treasure was followed by silver- and gold-rich mines in Nevada, Arizona, and part of Colorado taken from Mexico.

Colonel Sterling Price must have been satisfied that his rescue effort in New Mexico had benefitted the American economy greatly. But the slavery dispute that had originated the war with Mexico served as a training ground for officers on both sides in the Civil War. In a situation analogous to that of Virginian Robert E. Lee, Price was more loyal to his state of Missouri than to the United States. Although he had not favored Missouri secession, Price was infuriated when federal troops prevented it (Missouri was represented in the Confederate congress). He became Confederate States of America General Sterling Price.

General Price led frequently successful battles against the Federals in Arkansas and Missouri until he finally was forced to retreat by great numbers of Union troops. Price never did surrender to the Union but retreated with his battered, yet very competent, soldiers as far south as Mexico. There, he offered his support to Emperor Maximilian I of Mexico, a European nobleman. Napoleon III had convinced the emperor that the Mexican people desired his rule over them instead of recently elected president Benito Juarez, and he supplied French troops to support the naive Mexican emperor.

Most European nations recognized France's puppet emperor in Mexico, but the United States stuck by Juarez. In the midst of a great civil war, the United States could do little about the French invasion of Mexico. But when the Civil War ended, America was temporarily the strongest military power on earth and looking south with severe disapproval. The French left.

The puppet emperor refused the service of Price's veteran Confederate army. Mexico had outlawed slavery decades before Lincoln emancipated slaves after the Battle of Antietam in Maryland. The United States had always supported Mexico's elected president and might be distinctly displeased by a never-surrendered Confederate army just beyond its southern border. Or perhaps Maximilian still believed the lie fed to him by Napoleon III that the Mexican people loved their European emperor. Having refused the support of Price's veteran army, Maximilian was captured by the Mexicans, stood against an adobe wall, and shot to death.

Mexico killed Price less quickly. He was beset by diarrhea. Incapacitated, he returned to his circle of Missouri friends, who could not rescue him. He died of Mexican diarrhea twenty years after rescuing the Americans in New Mexico.

Searchers Rescued

In July 1868 Superintendent of Indian Affairs Thomas Murphy decided to hold back arms and ammunition promised to the Cheyenne the previous year in the Medicine Lodge Treaty. This peace agreement had been signed in Kansas by various Cheyenne leaders, including Tall Bull. Tall Bull then led a raid on a village of the Kaw, or Kansa, tribe, for generations the enemies of the Cheyenne.

To Murphy, using promised weapons to kill other Indians instead of bison seemed contrary to the terms of the peace treaty. Whatever his confusion about the terms of the Medicine Lodge Treaty, Tall Bull had no intention of giving up his historic right to kill Native farmers like the Kaw. Other Cheyenne were willing to keep the peace but were obdurate about receiving the promised guns and bullets. And they had allies among Euro-Americans who thought that peace and harmony would be served best by living up to the letter of the treaty.

Murphy eventually gave in and ordered distribution of arms according to the Medicine Lodge Treaty at Fort Larned in Kansas on August 9, 1868. But Tall Bull and his elite band of Cheyenne Dog Soldiers knew nothing of the federal government's change in policy because Tall Bull had already set out to attack another farming tribe, the Pawnee. On the way, however, the Dog Soldiers grew increasingly angry with the government's refusal to deliver arms promised by the treaty just because the Cheyenne were going to use them to kill other Native Americans in addition to hunting wildlife.

They forgot about the Pawnee and struck, instead, against white farming settlements in western Kansas and eastern Colorado. In two days, the Cheyenne killed fifteen men, raped five women, burned homes, and stole

This pistol in the Eagle Plume Collection along Colorado Highway 7 near Rocky Mountain National Park looks very similar to those issued to the 10th Cavalry who rescued searchers at Beecher Island.

stock. In response, Major George Forsyth led a patrol of fifty experienced civilian plainsmen (about half Civil War veterans from both sides) that he had recruited to search for hostile horse nomads, discourage their raids, and rescue any white captives the scouts might encounter.

On September 17, 1868, the scouts ran into six to seven hundred Cheyenne Dog Soldiers and southern Oglala Sioux a short distance west of the Kansas-Colorado boundary along the Arikaree Fork of the Republican River. Civilian scout Louis McLaughlin later wrote that following the trail from a wagon train attack where two teamsters had been killed led to an ever-growing trail of Cheyenne estimated by some to number nearly one thousand warriors. McLaughlin recalled that many of Forsyth's men thought this immense number should cause the scouts to retreat while they could.

The Cheyenne, among the deadliest mounted fighters in the world, attacked the scouts, who dug cover on an island in the nearly dry river—scant protection when outnumbered more than twelve to one. The scouts, however, were armed with seven-shot Spencer repeating rifles. The

Cheyenne had started on their raid in anger because they had not received the arms they felt were due them. Evidently, the Dog Soldiers were correct about the inferiority of their own weapons because they could not overrun and destroy all the island's defenders.

A very prominent Cheyenne warrior called Roman Nose at first had not joined the fight because he recently had learned that, while visiting with Sioux allies, he unknowingly had broken his private protective medicine policy by eating bread touched by an iron fork that Euro-Americans had made. Therefore, Roman Nose believed that joining in the attack would condemn him to death.

Any Dog Soldier had the right to act or refrain from acting in any way he chose. But the absence of so prestigious a warrior as Roman Nose seemed to be having a bad effect. He was taunted by another Cheyenne, named White Contrary, until Roman Nose agreed to join the next charge. Tall Bull urged him to wait at least until a purification ceremony could be performed. But Roman Nose's pride forbade that he wait before attacking the scouts, even though he was sure he would die. He did.

The death of Roman Nose and other warriors discouraged further mounted charges, and the Cheyenne settled down to lay siege to the scouts. The scouts suffered serious casualties: six fatalities and sixteen wounded. Forsyth was wounded three times. All their horses and mules were killed. For five days of siege, the scouts had to eat rotting horses and dig in the sand for water.

However, two pairs of messengers managed to slip by the surrounding Cheyenne and walk ninety miles to Fort Wallace in Kansas. Meanwhile, impatient horse nomads tired of laying siege (it was boring) and left the battle site after the fifth day. Forsyth had no way to know how many might be left to wipe out his scouts. On the ninth day, when the searchers were nearly out of ammunition and otherwise diminished in fighting shape, 10th Cavalry rescuers arrived to drive off any remaining hostiles and transport the wounded to medical aid. Former Union and Confederate soldiers among the scouts welcomed the African-American horse soldiers of the 10th Cavalry with tears of joy.

Unsurprisingly, both sides came to refer to the fight by the name of one who died. To horse nomads, it was the Fight Where Roman Nose Was Killed. The Euro-Americans called it the Battle of Beecher's Island, after second-in-command Frederick Beecher, who was slain there. The army decided that recruiting civilian scouts was not an effective way to discourage horse nomad raids.

Frederick Beecher was the nephew of famous abolitionist Henry Ward Beecher. Having strongly furthered the end of slavery, this clergyman helped organize the United States Indian Commission to encourage "the protection and elevation of Indians." The year after the Beecher Island fight, the commission strongly urged action of President Grant and Congress that influenced Grant's peace policy of "conquest by kindness."

Summit Springs

Among the survivors of Major George Forsyth's civilian scouts at the Beecher's Island fight were Tom Alderdice and Eli Zeigler, brothers-in-law and homesteaders in central Kansas. On May 30, 1869, less than a year after Beecher's Island, Tall Bull's Cheyenne hit a new settlement of farmers at Spillman Creek. Fifteen raiders encountered Zeigler and another brother-in-law driving a wagon. The brothers-in-law fled to cover in a creek bed, protected by the banks from Cheyenne sniping. Unwilling to repeat the charges of the previous fall in northeastern Colorado, the Cheyenne contented themselves with taking the wagon's horses.

The Cheyenne killed various other farmers and took captive one of their wives, Marie Weichel. About 5:00 p.m. the same day, they encountered Tom Alderdice's wife, Susanna. (Tom was buying supplies in Salina, about thirty-five miles away.) They shot and left for dead three of Susanna's sons, aged two, four, and five years. The four-year-old, though pierced by five arrows and two bullets, survived. The Cheyenne took Susanna along with her eight-month-old daughter. This tragedy awaited Tom Alderdice when he arrived back from Salina the next day.

On June 1, Alderdice set out alone to search for and rescue his wife and daughter. Following the raiders' trail, he caught up with them but decided that he could not achieve a rescue alone. He rode to Fort Leavenworth, where he encountered Lieutenant Colonel George Custer and his wife, Libbie. Custer was there to judge a horse show. Libbie later described Alderdice in her book *Following the Guidon* as "nearly a madman as can be. His eyes wild, frenzied, and sunken with grief, his tear-stained face—all told a terrible tale of what he had and was enduring."

This steel-tipped Cheyenne arrow and bow with sinew string are similar to those that pierced but failed to kill Tom and Susanna Alderdice's four-year-old son during an 1869 raid in Kansas.

Alderdice's own account of his search for his wife and baby and a description of Susanna were forwarded by Fort Leavenworth officers to Major Eugene Carr, who already was searching with his cavalry and a force of Pawnee scouts for Tall Bull. Alderdice returned to his solitary search and discovered an abandoned Cheyenne camp. There he found his eight-month-old baby Alice, strangled to death by a bowstring, presumably because she made too much noise crying during the hardship of traveling with the raiders. All Alderdice could do was cry and pray that Major Carr could rescue Susanna.

On June 9, Major Carr led eight companies of the 5th Cavalry and three companies of Pawnee scouts as well as Buffalo Bill Cody on a hunt for the captives. (Cody arrived from a Wild West show and took over scouting duties despite a lack of authority to do so.) There followed a series of battles and skirmishes along the Republican River valley. In these fights, Corporal John Kile and Pawnee Sergeant Mad Bear won Medals of Honor. Tall Bull, with a village of approximately eighty tipis was headed north to join with other hostile Cheyenne in Wyoming. He did not make it.

On July 9, Carr rode his fighters hard to catch Tall Bull's Dog Soldiers before they could cross the South Platte River. On the evening of July 10,

Carr recognized that his horses were wearing out. He reduced his force to those who had mounts that remained fit for a hard ride. With 244 cavalrymen, 50 Pawnee, and Buffalo Bill, Carr's force set out to circle around the Cheyenne some thirty-five miles and attack from an unexpected direction in northeast Colorado near the present town of Sterling. It worked . . . sort of.

Three companies wide, a bugle-triggered charge about 2:00 p.m. on July 11 hit the Cheyenne camp. The Pawnee were particularly adept and eager when it came to killing horse nomads who had raided easy-to-find Pawnee villages—near their agricultural fields—for generations.

The fog of battle confused later accounts. Buffalo Bill took credit for killing Tall Bull; so did Major Frank North, who had recruited the Pawnee scouts. Carr credited Private David Mann, who was said to have seized Tall Bull's favorite horse after he shot the chief. This contradicts Indian testimony that Tall Bull was in the process of escaping with his favorite wife and daughter when he turned around to face the soldiers and Pawnee. He was said to have rallied nineteen other warriors, shot his own horse through the mouth as an acceptance of death, and died fighting the Pawnee in a gully. In fact, the confusion about who killed Tall Bull might have been due to unfamiliarity with his appearance. Few Euro-Americans or Pawnee who saw him close enough to recognize him lived to experience a second encounter.

After the battle, the army found one of Tall Bull's wives and a child sitting on a nearby hillside. The soldiers sent them along with seventeen other noncombatants up the Missouri River to join friends.

Aware that vengeful soldiers and Pawnee might find their camp, the Cheyenne had placed their two women captives at separate ends of the village, intending to kill both if an attack came. Maria Weichel happened to be near where the cavalry rode in. Although shot, she was rescued. A war club crushed Susanna Alderdice's skull. She died just as her attempted rescuers reached her. An army doctor did what he could to repair her appearance. (There were no casualties on his side to treat.) The cavalry buried her in a still-unknown grave at the battle site, which Carr wanted to name Susanna Springs, but it already had the name of Summit Springs.

Search for Some, Rescue Others

In the 1870s the United States government tried to reduce a basic difference between Euro-Americans and Native Americans on the Great Plains. Euro-American society governed itself through elected representatives authorized to make decisions that members of their society were obligated (or forced) to follow. Native American societies governed themselves through consensus, whereby decisions agreed to by every member were the only decisions that each member of the society was obligated to obey. The largest and most influential plains tribe was the Sioux, many of whom respected the leadership of Sitting Bull from the 1860s through the 1880s.

In 1874 gold turned up in the Black Hills, part of the Great Sioux Reservation (all of present South Dakota west of the Missouri River) outlined in the Treaty of 1868, which many Sioux did not recognize as imperative for individuals. The federal government tried to keep invading Euro-American prospectors separate from treaty-ignoring Sioux, such as Sitting Bull, by purchasing the Black Hills. The notion of selling the Black Hills to the Euro-Americans was unacceptable or unintelligible to most Sioux because that unique high point in the plains was a treasured source of food, tipi poles, and spiritual support.

Euro-Americans, who understood the Sioux's love for the Black Hills, believed that the Sioux could be persuaded to accept substitute values, mainly money. And some prominent Sioux were willing to sell, arguing over the price. For Euro-Americans, in contrast, there was no substitute for Black Hills gold in the wake of severe economic hard times brought on by the recently ended Civil War.

The Civil War had resulted from Euro-Americans being unable to make representative government work in a way consistent with their concept of "all men are created equal." The renewed representative government wanted to include Native Americans in their "all men are created equal" system, but this required that Native Americans conform to Euro-American Christian culture, including a farming-based economy and representative government.

Most Sioux did not find this inclusion in Euro-American society to be appealing. The only encounters they wanted with Euro-Americans were to obtain guns, ammunition, and various other manufactured goods. Therefore, after the Treaty of 1868, Sioux society divided into three factions within each of the named bands.

One group was willing to live on the Great Sioux Reservation despite bureaucratic inefficiency and sometimes corruption in delivering to reservation Sioux the goods that had been promised to them in return for their giving up their independence. Another Sioux group chose to spend hard northern plains winters living on the federal dole on reservations and dwelling during the warm summer months on the wide plains, including the unceded Indian territory in today's Wyoming, then mostly empty of Euro-Americans. There they could hunt bison and other animals as well as kill their traditional enemies among other tribes such as the Crow, Shoshone, or Arikara. Perhaps a third of the Sioux, including the admired Sitting Bull and Crazy Horse, lived all year in the unceded territory and rejected all contact with Euro-Americans (except traders, of course). Sitting Bull commanded enough respect to hold together many Sioux bands to a significant degree for united action against enemy tribes and (initially less important) Euro-Americans.

The authority that Sitting Bull managed to exercise became semi-formalized by a council of bands held along Rosebud Creek, near the present Wyoming-Montana border in 1869. His proclamation of authority was a unique revolution among the consensus-minded Sioux (as well as their northern Cheyenne allies). Despite his prestige, and even with the aid of self-appointed policing organizations called *akicita*, Sitting Bull had trouble enforcing discipline he deemed necessary for the benefit of the Sioux.

Euro-American leaders also had political problems. Some of their constituents wanted to build peaceful relations with Native Americans, even with those who did not reciprocate this goodwill. Other constituents wanted Black Hills gold shoveled into the American economy.

In late 1875 the federal government secretly sided with the gold-seekers. They claimed it was necessary to enforce the Treaty of 1868, which many Sioux had not signed, did not recognize as authoritative, or did not bother to consider at all. Early in 1876 the Euro-Americans attempted to send runners to all free-roaming Native Americans. All the tribes, the message proclaimed, must report to reservations in an impossibly short time (given the difficulty of winter travel), quit fighting other tribes, and change to a representative form of government (so that the federal government could bargain with chiefs who had authority to sell the Black Hills). Any bands that did not comply with the summons would be considered hostile to the United States and subject to army attack.

Euro-American justification for this decree was raiding by some non-reservation Sioux on Montanans along the upper Yellowstone River and against friendly Native tribes, such as the Crow and Arikara. Indeed, the unceded territory Sioux, such as Sitting Bull and Crazy Horse, had been taking part in such raids together with Cheyenne allies, but they and others in anarchistic Sioux society failed to understand why such generations-old practices should be upsetting to the Euro-Americans. The messages carried to Native villages through bitter winter cold seemed more puzzling than threatening.

Euro-American motivation became irrelevant in mid-March 1876, when US cavalry attacked a village that had not reported to a reservation as directed. The attack was largely a failure from the cavalry perspective, but it motivated the Sioux to unite in all-out war under the leadership of Sitting Bull. In June free-roaming bands together with a few winter-on-the-reservation Sioux assembled near Rosebud Creek. Deciding along with Crazy Horse that battle should be delayed until all reservation allies could arrive, Sitting Bull urged this accumulation of perhaps a thousand warriors to leave the Euro-American troops alone unless there was an army attack.

Scouts reported that just such an army was approaching from the south. It was commanded by General George Crook, whose competent leadership had allowed him to achieve his rank when most army officers had been demoted from their Civil War ranks due to deep cuts in the federal army after the war. Part of Crook's successful Indian-fighting effort was to recruit Native auxiliaries, who had been fighting enemy Native Americans for at least a century. During his search to force Sioux now declared hostile onto a reservation, Crook recruited about 350 Sioux enemies among the Shoshone and Crow. Although not necessarily friendly toward each other, these tribes bitterly hated the powerful Sioux, against whom they had countless scores to settle.

Crow and Shoshone scouts prevented a surprise attack by Sioux and Cheyenne down this slope above Rosebud Creek.

After a dawn start on June 17, 1876, Crook called for a rest stop at mid-morning so that his men could quench their coffee addiction along Rosebud Creek. Not a coffee drinker himself, Crook rested by playing cards with his officers, while the Shoshone and Crow, not having volunteered for a picnic and games, searched ahead for enemy Sioux.

The previous night, the young Sioux warriors (plus a few older ones) grew excited by the approach of their enemies. Striking them would provide opportunity for praise and plunder. Sitting Bull and Crazy Horse, although fierce and highly respected warriors, tried to command the young warriors to delay attacking the soldiers until winter-on-the-reservation Sioux arrived in force to double the number of Sioux fighters.

Of course, the young warriors followed the traditional course and ignored their supposed leaders. They did not want to wait to share the glory and plunder with their reservation brethren. Even the *akicita* could not keep these eager young fighters from sneaking from camp at night with the intention of attacking Crook the next day (June 19 by the Euro-American calendar). Sitting Bull and Crazy Horse, realizing that, as usual, the young warriors were going to do as they pleased, gave up the notion of strategic command. Sitting Bull, having recently endured self-torture for sacrifice and mystic vision, was temporarily unfit for combat. Crazy Horse agreed to lead a surprise attack against Crook from tablelands above Rosebud Creek down a gully leading to the army's coffee break.

The 350-some Crow and Shoshone fighters on reaching the top of the gully encountered approximately 1,000 Sioux (plus allied Cheyenne) fighters. The Shoshone and Crow searching for Sioux spoiled the surprise attack and raced back to warn Crook, thereby rescuing the army from at least extensive casualties. Fueled by the same fury that fueled the Sioux, the Crow and Shoshone fought ferociously against awful odds until the soldiers could form a defense.

Likely the Native Americans on both sides were better fighters than the Euro-Americans, but each Native American fought as an individual whereas Crook's men were disciplined to fight as a unit. Discipline successfully opposed individual skill as the generally back-and-forth fight formed into three major skirmishes. Finally, Sioux and Cheyenne warriors decided they had achieved enough individual glory, although scant plunder, and left the battle. The Cheyenne remembered the fight as Where the Girl Saved Her Brother, for Buffalo Calf Woman rode through the battle to extract her brother, Comes-in-Sight, whose horse had been shot.

Crook decided that he had won the battle because he remained on the field. The Sioux decided they had won the battle because Crook had remained on the field and no longer was advancing toward the Sioux. Everyone agreed that the Crow and Shoshone fighters had prevented a major Sioux victory by rescuing Crook's force after successfully searching for the Sioux and holding them off until the Euro-Americans were ready to fight (and presumably had finished their coffee break).

Crook returned south to his supply base because his troops had used up too much ammunition to continue to advance. They had been disciplined to fight as a unit, but Congress had not allotted funds for practice ammunition. They were terrible shots, expending approximately one thousand bullets for each Sioux killed.

Crook therefore could not link his forces as planned with the cavalry commanded by George Custer, who six days after the Rosebud battle, of which he knew nothing, led 691 soldiers against thousands of Sioux and Cheyenne warriors along the Little Bighorn River. The winter-on-the-reservation Sioux for whom Sitting Bull had wanted to wait before attacking Crook at Rosebud Creek had arrived at the Little Bighorn.

Search and Partial Rescue

———

Major Joel Elliott and eighteen cavalrymen rode in pursuit of Cheyenne Indians fleeing on foot, who might have had with them Clara and Willie Blinn, a white woman and toddler. Elliott shouted that he would get either a promotion or a coffin. He did not get a promotion. When his commanding officer, Lieutenant Colonel George Custer, who led the search and rescue mission, finally discovered the mutilated remains of Elliott's troop the following month along the Washita River in today's Oklahoma, the point of a coffin might have seemed dubious.

Clara and Willie were killed as soon as Custer attacked the Washita winter village where the Blinns, captured in southeastern Colorado, were being held. The cavalry did manage to rescue two Kansas women captives. Custer's force, led by Osage Indian scouts, had trailed the Kansans' captors (a large war party of some 150 raiders) through a November 1868 blizzard. The search brought cavalry to the Cheyenne camp after midnight November 26. Custer divided his force into four groups to attack simultaneously early the next morning.

Custer did not know that the chief who was the theoretical leader of this camp was Black Kettle, the most prominent peace advocate among the Cheyenne. However, wise Black Kettle had little real authority in the mostly anarchic society that typified horse nomads. Young men wanted prestige, wealth, and sex. For more than a century after the introduction of Spanish horses from the south and French guns from the north, horse nomad bands sought these goals through raiding other societies, first Indian farmers whom they could find in permanent villages near their agricultural fields, and later Euro-American farmers whose homesteads were equally easy to find. Chiefs like Black Kettle had no more power to stop raiders than mayors of modern cities can stop the violence of teen gangs.

Cavalry bullets killed Black Kettle and his wife along the Washita. The Osage scouts, happy with the destruction of their traditional enemies, stayed well away from the attack for the reasonable fear that they would be mistaken for hostile Cheyenne and shot by the soldiers. It was a danger risked by all Native scouts among US army forces on the Great Plains.

The army found plunder from raids on homesteaders in the soon-destroyed Cheyenne camp along with the rescued women. Also discovered was the presence of many other winter camps along the Washita, from which warriors were approaching, drawn by the sound of gunfire from Black Kettle's village. Unexpectedly outnumbered, Custer led his troops in a pretend attack on the other villages, which sent the approaching warriors back to protect their families. Custer then retreated north with fifty-three Cheyenne women and children as hostages, thereby forestalling attack by pursuing warriors.

During all this fighting furor, Custer did not know what had become of second-in-command Major Elliott and his men. Some of Custer's officers were frantic to search for Elliot. Custer maintained that Elliott perhaps had gotten lost and would turn up eventually. Or, if he had run into a hoard of the best horse warriors in the world, Elliott already was dead. With a human shield of Cheyenne noncombatants, Custer extricated his soldiers and the two rescued women from a very bad military situation and retreated north through bitter cold weather.

Even more bitter was the reaction of eastern advocates for Native Americans, who condemned the Washita fight as butchery of innocent Indians by a glory-hungry soldier seeking to boost his career (Custer). This claim is still heard today. The army found the bodies of a murdered mother and toddler, two rescued women who might begin to recover from a fate-worse-than-death experience, and tipis along the Washita holding booty from raids on farming communities. Therefore, the army ignored criticism and continued to search the southern plains for white female captives to rescue, and shrugged off the death of peace martyr Black Kettle as collateral damage.

But the loss of Major Elliott's soldiers could not be shrugged off, especially after Custer discovered the bodies of Elliott's troop on a second mission that used diplomacy as well as bullets to rescue two more homesteader women. Anger over the supposed abandonment of the major raged furiously among Custer's officers and through the rest of the army. Custer's career was seriously damaged.

Most outraged among officers in the Washita fight was Captain Frederick Benteen, who wrote a letter to the *St. Louis Democrat* published on February 9, 1869: "But surely some search will be made for our missing comrades. No, they were forgotten. Over them . . . the wolves will hold high carnival, and their howling will be their only requiem." The letter was reprinted in the *New York Times* and *Chicago Tribune*. Custer threatened violence against Benteen, but their hatred for each other never progressed to dueling. Failure to search for and rescue his men caused Custer to fall far in military esteem.

However, General "Fighting Phil" Sheridan, who was directly in charge of subduing hostile horse nomads, saw in his subordinate Custer the same heroic competence that the young cavalry officer had shown fighting Confederates at Gettysburg and many subsequent battles in Virginia. When Sheridan had an "Indian problem," he called on Custer to help fix it.

The Indian problem that arose on the northern plains had a different cause from the southern plains war, but cavalry activity was mostly the same. On June 25, 1876, Custer led the 7th Cavalry to search for Sioux villages along the Little Bighorn River in today's Montana. His goal was not to rescue white captives, but to force unwilling Sioux onto a reservation in South Dakota and Nebraska. However, these roaming bison hunters were joined on the Little Bighorn by masses of Sioux who spent the harsh winter on their reservation, eating from the federal dole until warm summer weather sent them from the reservation to the pleasures of hunting and war. They were also joined by similarly motivated Cheyenne and Arapaho.

As on the Washita, Custer's search for the roaming Sioux led to many more Indians than he had reason to expect when he set out from Fort Abraham Lincoln near Bismarck, North Dakota. Instead of riding through the single-digit temperatures of November, he was pursuing "hostiles" through the triple-digit temperatures of June. He had pushed his horses (and soldiers) through sleepless night and intense morning heat because, in perhaps one of the greatest ironies of American history, he feared the Indians would elude his search. On such battered steeds retreat was impossible.

Custer was outnumbered seven to one by superb warriors who were rested, very highly motivated (to protect their families), and better armed for close combat than were his troopers (the Sioux had legally acquired Winchester and Springfield repeating rifles, which they would use against the cavalry's single-shot carbines, more deadly from a distance). It seems impossible to imagine a worse military situation. But Custer, still unaware of his awful fix, again divided his force into four units to surround the Indians. He sent one unit under Captain Benteen to the upper part of the Little Bighorn Valley, which was out of sight, to attack or block the flight of Indians that might be there. As it turned out, there were none. Another unit, in reserve, carried ammunition and other supplies.

Custer ordered his second-in-command, Major Marcus Reno, to attack the southernmost village, the only village they could see along the river. Custer promised Reno support, but then headed north up ragged bluffs above the river and village where he spotted some Indians, who then disappeared by the time he got there. Evidently, Custer changed his mind and set out to attack and contain the Indians from the other (still not visible) end of their camp.

Whether or not this was the kind of support Reno expected, he led his troopers in a surprise attack on the village. Before he got there, he met a wall of Sioux, formed a skirmish line, and was quickly driven into a retreat to another position. With Indians swarming through his ranks, he retreated again for the top of the bluff where Custer had gone. When Reno's unit managed to scramble up the bluff under heavy, deadly fire, by luck they joined with the unit hauling supplies and with Captain Benteen's men, who had found no Indians to fight. Soon plenty of Indians found them. But then the Sioux/Cheyenne attack slackened, allowing the Reno/Benteen units to fashion a sort of defense position on the hill.

Word had spread among the fighting Sioux and Cheyenne that more soldiers were attacking the north end of the line of camps along the river. When Custer reached the top of the river bluffs, he had seen for the first time the expanse of the Native camps. If it did not appear that all the Indians in the world were there, then at least all of their best warriors were present and in the process of destroying Reno's command.

No one who might have heard Custer's comment at this time lived to report it. But Custer was famous in the army for, among other things, his disinclination to swear. Assuming that he remained consistent in this regard, it would not be remarkable if the word that popped into his head on looking down at Reno's fight was "Elliott!" Just by the number of troopers threatened with massacre, the Reno plight would be six or seven times worse than the Elliott destruction that had so damaged Custer's career.

Custer had not rescued Elliott, but he set out to rescue Reno. As on the Washita, he could attack part of the village across the river at the base of the bluffs. The village seemed emptied of warriors, all drawn to fight Reno. Custer could capture a large number of women and children as human shields and prevent further Indian attack.

But the terrain was very different from Oklahoma. The Little Bighorn had cut its way through a valley, forming steep and rugged bluffs, much less suited to cavalry than the relatively placid Washita. And the mounted soldiers could splash through the Little Bighorn to the Indian camp only at widely separated fords.

Custer sent two companies of his unit under Captain George Yates (about eighty men in an army typically understaffed by a Civil War–weary nation) down a steep and ragged gully to the river, across from the camp. According to Cheyenne oral history, ten warriors who had not yet made ready to respond to Reno's surprise attack managed to hold off Yates's troopers long enough for most of the other warriors to stream down from the Reno fight to protect their families.

Custer waited above for Yates's report while expecting reinforcements for his five total companies to be provided by Benteen and the supply unit. Custer's youngest brother, Boston, had been with the supply unit and had

This memorial, like others scattered across the Little Bighorn National Battlefield but unlike the national cemetery at the battlefield, indicates where a Cheyenne warrior died but not where his body was laid to rest.

raced ahead to join his brothers George and Tom to get in on the glory, bringing with him the news that Benteen was not far behind. Unknown to any of the Custers, Benteen had halted to rescue the very beleaguered Reno.

Custer likely had sent Yates to search the river for a crossing point. Or he might have been staging a false attack on the camp to draw the mass of warriors away from the counterattack against Reno, similar to the false attack that had diverted counterattack by a superior Indian force along the Washita. In any case, army presence across the river from the northernmost camp succeeded in rescuing Reno's unit.

The Reno/Benteen units, however, also suffered heavy casualties in a desperate two-day siege that yielded nineteen Congressional Medal of Honor winners on what came to be known as Reno Hill. Rescue arrived with another large army unit that also had been searching for Sioux. Before the siege began in earnest, Reno/Benteen soldiers tried futilely to break through masses of Sioux and Cheyenne to rescue Custer, as Benteen had urged Custer to search for and rescue Elliott. As with Elliott, the attempt likely was already too late.

Yates almost certainly reported to Custer that the river could be crossed and hostages captured. But hundreds of Sioux and Cheyenne warriors who had abandoned Reno arrived to suddenly turn Custer's offense into defensive disaster. The wipeout was quick. The Custer family lost three brothers, a nephew, and a brother-in-law.

The 265 casualties at the Battle of the Little Bighorn were negligible compared to the massive bloodletting of the relatively recent Civil War battles. But Civil War hero Custer had been killed in the nation's most famous defeat. A motion picture scholar might be able to count all the movies about Custer's Last Stand, but the total of printed accounts surely is beyond reckoning.

Like Elliott, whose death had cursed Custer's career, the 7th Cavalry's commander did not get a promotion. Although many of his troopers on Last Stand Hill were mutilated beyond recognition, Custer's corpse remained comparatively intact, or so everybody claimed. He did get a coffin.

LIONS AND GRIZZLIES AND BLACK BEARS

Lion in Wait

On January 14, 1991, a male high school athlete was on the first lap of a conditioning run that he had planned with his coach around his school in Idaho Springs, Colorado, in the mountains. On a section of that lap, he knew his fellow students in a classroom could see him run by. To impress them with his humor, he began to run wobbly legged with his arms flailing in the air, seeming altogether out of control. His scheme worked. Some of his fellow students smiled or even chuckled. To them he looked funny.

To the mountain lion that had been stalking him on his regular route, he looked vulnerable with his sudden wobbly run, easy to catch. Before the athlete finished a full circuit around his school, but out of sight of the windows, the cougar struck from behind. The kill was quick, and the lion dragged the runner away to eat.

When the runner failed to come home that evening, his mother called his friends and then the sheriff. Sheriff's deputies cornered the runner's friends the next day in school to find out where the runner had gone. (He had not been enthusiastic about the non-athletic aspects of high school.) The friends denied that they knew anything. A teacher intervened, maintaining that the athlete did not skip town: He cared nothing for grades; he only cared about bike racing, and his custom-made bicycle was still at home. The students in the class for whose amusement the runner had pretended wobbling remembered that he had not gone by on his usual second circuit.

Impromptu searches began around the high school with the runner's friends yelling his name. Of course, that did not work. The sheriff called in

A mountain lion watches prey.

trained searchers to cover the area where the runner normally jogged. The Alpine Rescue Team, expert volunteers who searched for missing hikers and skiers in the Colorado mountain wilderness, arrived to set up operations in the mountain town. Standing in winter clothing around their search and rescue truck, they planned how to find the lost jogger.

No one considered that he might have become mountain lion prey because lions were considered to be very shy of humans. Never before had a lion killed any human in Colorado, although another jogger had a very close call, saved by a deer that wandered by, providing more convenient prey. Formerly inhabitants of the wild, some lions had become urbanized in pursuit of deer that residents of mountain towns protected from human hunters, perhaps reasoning that hunters might kill humans accidentally.

Urbanized lions learned to ignore millennia of deadly natural selection and became unafraid of people and their wolf cousins, dogs. One lion even learned to lose the fear of dogs and saw them as prey, instead of predators on lions. Though that lion was killed, the threat remained that if one lion learned to prey on dogs, others might learn to prey on humans. But the searchers never considered lion predation because it never had happened before in Colorado.

Rather, they coordinated their usual techniques to find the lost. They divided the search area into grids on a topographic map and sketched the runner's normal route, marked where he had last been seen, and divided adjacent hills and gullies into an irregular pattern. Each division, ranging between twenty and fifty acres, received a number.

The search then proceeded into phases, with more detailed searches occurring with each phase. First, they started with the most expeditious search in hope of finding the runner quickly. Search dogs were brought in, given the runner's moccasin to sniff as a scent article, and taken where the runner had last been seen. Of course, he ran that route daily, and his scent flooded the area. A bloodhound led searchers to a parking lot that his regular run crossed, and some people thought he had gotten into a car and skipped town. A bloodhound's nose is so sensitive that it can follow people inside a car, but the runner's scent was everywhere.

Meanwhile, small human groups, called "hasty teams," checked linear areas along streams, trails, and roads, calling the runner's name. This was similar to what the runner's friends already had done with the same futility.

In the afternoon, stage two began. Searchers tramping about seventy-five feet apart ranged across the countryside, marching through and across any obstacle, looking for some clue to the runner's presence. By the time dusk arrived before 5:00 p.m., Alpine Rescue Team leaders began to think they were on a "bastard search," trying to find someone who was not present. This was, in a sense, true. For safety's sake, they gave up searching until morning.

That night, the runner's family and comrades were puzzled. His mother thought he had been hit by a car and was lying in a ditch. His father thought he had been kidnapped. A teacher feared the runner had fallen down a mine shaft left over from the town's founding. A friend contemplated alien abduction.

The next morning, Alpine Search and Rescue broke one of its own rules and accepted help from local, untrained volunteers under team supervision. Usually, well-intended but untrained volunteers are deemed a hazard to a successful search: They get mixed up, or they become lost, or they get hurt. But this town's terrain was considered safe enough that the townsfolk's help was accepted. With more searchers, the effort began again, expanding to everywhere anyone could contemplate.

This was stage three. Alpine Rescue Team leaders had decided that the runner likely was not to be found near his high school. But they needed to be sure by trying one more time, using a line search.

In a line search, at least six searchers line up along a boundary of a search area. They stand no more than twenty feet apart, normally much closer. Each searcher must be able to see everything up to each adjacent searcher. On the end of the line, a searcher holds a compass and walks slowly ahead, watching the compass needle to keep everyone walking along a constant bearing. They look into trees, around boulders, under logs. At the opposite end of the search area, the line of searchers moves together either left or right, does an about-face, and walks in the opposite direction. Their only comfort in this tedious practice is that they are not mowing a lawn, which the search resembles.

The tedium is increased by the belief that they are looking for nothing. Rather, they are making sure that there is nothing to be found. But in this case, there was.

On the presumed final sweep, searchers saw the runner's corpse beneath a large Rocky Mountain juniper tree, a species with branches normally growing all the way to the ground. They assumed the runner had been murdered in a ghastly fashion. His chest was laid open and most of his internal organs were removed. His face was peeled away with only the skull staring with empty eye sockets into the cold air.

This was a horrible crime. No one considered a mountain lion because never before had a lion killed anyone in Colorado. Even when they saw the lion squatting amid other junipers about fifteen feet away, they did not associate the cat with the runner's death. Rather, they considered the cougar's presence to be a complication at a murder scene, until the cat began defending its prey. Reconsidering the humans that surrounded it, the cat ran over a hill. Searchers scattered to get out of its path. When the lion began to circle back toward its kill, a local SWAT sniper shot and killed it.

A subsequent necropsy of the lion found remains of the runner's organs in its digestive system. The lion had been a perfectly healthy young male, like his victim.

Guarding Prey

———

To a ten-year-old boy near the town of Grand Lake in July 1997, a hike to Cascade Falls in Colorado's Rocky Mountain National Park was less interesting than the park's many types of wildlife. His parents let him leave a small pile of nuts alongside the trail to feed some small rodents. This was contrary to well-publicized park regulations, but it seemed a harmless infraction for a small boy with a child's immature reaction to the total aesthetic value of Rocky Mountain wilderness.

The boy was eager to return to his wildlife offering to see if it had been consumed. He never found out. Running down the trail after seeing the waterfall, two and a half miles from the trailhead and never out of his parents' sight for more than a couple of minutes, he was jumped by a mountain lion about 4:30 p.m.

His parents came upon him with his torso hidden in some trailside bushes; his legs and feet were still on the trail. They thought it was a joke. Then they saw the feline predator trying to drag him away.

The lion ran away when they charged it. The boy's mother, a nurse, began to administer cardiopulmonary resuscitation to her son while the father attempted to stop the bleeding from cuts and puncture wounds to the face, head, and neck. Soon another family, parents with an eight-year-old daughter, came down the trail. The mother in this group was also a nurse and began to aid in CPR. Her husband, ignoring any lion danger, ran down the trail to summon help. The second nurse thought she detected a faint pulse in the boy, but then it disappeared.

The nurses continued CPR for forty minutes until the first ranger arrived about 5:10 p.m., after a twenty-minute race from Grand Lake.

While the mothers continued CPR, he located a helicopter landing site in a nearby meadow.

Within fifteen minutes more help arrived—a county deputy sheriff, a ranger who was also an emergency medical technician, the director of Grand County Emergency Medical Services, and a paramedic. Soon another team arrived with a wheeled litter. After more than an hour of CPR with no success, the director of county medical services told the boy's parents that further CPR was unlikely to help. With their permission, cardiopulmonary resuscitation was halted at 5:37 p.m.

Some rangers and other search and rescue personnel escorted the families and transported the ten-year-old's body down to Grand Lake. Other rangers hurried up the Tonahutu Creek and North Inlet trails to warn other hikers about a dangerous lion. One ranger was left at the scene of the attack so that further examination of available evidence could be conducted the next day.

Meanwhile, the lion was not happy that her prey had been stolen before she had a chance to eat it. Mule deer, her typical prey, often grazed in the meadow. Perhaps she previously had killed a fawn there. Or perhaps she had been surprised by the ten-year-old boy running down the trail, and had pounced on the child as a startle reaction. In any case, she was hungry and frustrated.

At 7:17 p.m. the ranger guarding the site saw the lion, which had been unable to guard her kill, silently stalking him. She then crouched and launched her attack. The guard was an enforcement ranger, essentially a cop and armed for that role. He had pulled his sidearm when he saw the lion. As she shot toward him, he fired three shots at her from about fifteen feet. She was wounded and ran away. Hearing the shots, three other rangers showed up to reinforce the guard detail, anticipating that the lion would soon be tracked and killed.

A half hour later, two more rangers came up the trail, escorting an experienced tracker and his pack of hounds. Lions regard the subspecies *Canis lupus familiaris* with the same dread with which they regard the gray wolf. Millennia of natural selection have favored for survival those lions that instinctively feared their natural predator, the gray wolf, *Canis lupus*. With

A mountain lion prepares to launch an attack.

only 4 percent difference between the genetic makeup of wolves and their domestic dog descendants, wolves and dogs have been regarded as the same species since 1993. The rare lion that departs from Darwinian directives to regard dogs as prey rather than predator ends up getting shot and killed, thereby the deadly dictates of natural selection are reinforced. For lions, dogs mean death. Humans by themselves are lion prey, but humans with dogs are, by association, lion predators to be avoided. If a lion has learned that humans and dogs are usually found together, humans appear less palatable.

The tracker's hounds exactly fit the lion's stereotype, and they instantly picked up the lion's scent. They pursued and circled her, darting in to bite. By 8:00 p.m., within two hundred yards of the kill site, the lion fled up a tree from the hounds, which kept barking at her, circling her perch, and jumping with front feet against the trunk. Soon the rangers and the tracker joined the hounds below the tree.

The rangers shot and killed the lion and carried her body away for necropsy in Fort Collins at the Colorado State University College of Veterinary Medicine. The lion was approximately three years old. She was in good shape and had been pregnant for about forty-five days with three fetuses. It was unlikely that anything physical made her more likely than any other lion, normally shy of humans, to attack and kill a human child.

The National Park Service (NPS) barred hikers the next day from the North Inlet Trail that ran past Cascade Falls. The morning after the lion and human fatalities, the tracker with an NPS escort returned with his dogs (trained to distinguish between the scents of two lions). The dogs decreed that there was no second lion. The attacking lion had been typically alone.

The Grand County Coroner performed an autopsy on the ten-year-old victim. He had not died of bites or claw cuts, none of which would have been fatal. Rather, he suffocated on his own vomit brought up during the attack.

The hiking family had walked past a sign posted at the trailhead by NPS, which warned that a lion had been reported in the area. If they read it, they were completely reasonable in continuing their hike to Cascade Falls. Lions are so uncommon (perhaps five thousand throughout Colorado) and normally so disinclined to be around, let alone to attack, humans that the danger from encountering a lion while hiking was less than from driving a car to the trailhead. Statistics, of course, are scant solace to grieving parents or to search and rescue teams.

Garbage Bears

———

Grizzly bears play a much more conspicuous role in Rocky Mountain search and rescue missions than do black bears because grizzlies are individually more dangerous. Many injuries and deaths caused by grizzlies are due to the bears seeking human food, which causes some bears to follow the reasonable assumption that humans *are* food. (This is true also of black bear incidents, which has caused Rocky Mountain National Park to require that all wilderness campers carry commercial, hard-sided, bear-proof food containers between May 1 and November 1. Similar regulations govern human/bear interactions in other parks.)

Of particular concern to all bear researchers is the idea that grizzlies yearn for people food because they have been taught to add nutritious garbage to their diets by having access to human garbage dumps. In the 1970s, famous bear researcher Frank Craighead was in the midst of a dispute with Yellowstone National Park administrators about garbage-habituated grizzlies. Both Craighead and the National Park Service agreed that dump bears were aesthetically awful and posed an increased threat to humans. The dispute was how to remedy this situation. NPS already had taken steps to prevent grizzlies from feeding at garbage dumps within Yellowstone. In effect, they had said no. Dumps accessible to bears were eliminated.

Craighead agreed with that overall policy, but he feared that making the bears instantly give up garbage would increase bear-caused injuries and deaths among park visitors as the bears sought other sources of human food. Therefore, he maintained the bears should be weaned off garbage gradually. This also would protect the then-endangered grizzly population because bears that attacked people were often killed by NPS. The Park

A grizzly bear finds nourishment at a picnic table abandoned by humans for a good reason.

Service maintained that once they closed the park dumps to bears in 1970, they certainly were not going to reopen them at irregular intervals to gradually wean the bruins from garbage.

In June 1972 two hitchhikers received a ride into Yellowstone from a concessionaire employee, who let them out at Old Faithful with a warning about grizzlies and told them to check at the nearby ranger station for bear information. Instead, they carried their packs over the Old Faithful boardwalk and climbed into the woods above Grand Geyser to set up an illegal camp.

Subsequently, an acquaintance working at the Old Faithful Inn warned them that they were camped illegally. They ignored him and hung around for a night and a day. After a few drinks at the inn on the second night, they returned late to their camp and in the dark surprised an old female grizzly rooting through their unsecured food, an imitation of a garbage dump. The mutually frightened bear and men reacted in predictable ways, and one man became grizzly grub.

The other man ran with his friend's screams in his ears, fleeing across dark boardwalks, and miraculously failing to die in a scalding hot spring. He collapsed in the Old Faithful Inn, gasping that his friend had been attacked by a bear.

Rangers started at once to search for the missing illegal camper. Hidden among densely growing lodgepole pines in what often are called "doghair stands" for the closeness of the trunks, the campsite was hard to find in the dark. The rangers divided into search teams of three, keeping abreast with a ranger armed with a rifle or shotgun on the right or left and a ranger in the middle shining a flashlight. They had to fear not only a grizzly but also falling into a hot spring.

Fear and labor took their toll on the searchers' stamina until one accidentally fired his shotgun, blasting a hole into a boardwalk near another searcher's left foot. That searcher with a shotgun was done for the night and was escorted back to the Old Faithful Inn to lie down under supervision of a nurse.

At daybreak a ranger search and rescue team found the partially eaten camper. They trapped and killed the old bear and found remnants of the camper in her claws and digestive tract. She weighed only 232 pounds (light for a grizzly, perhaps due to her elderly footpads and teeth). Rangers could recognize her as a bear with a garbage-consumption history. Human presence around park boundaries nearly guarantees that grizzlies will continue to have access to refuse even after all sources of garbage within national parks have been eliminated.

Likely, grizzly bears have been garbage bears for more than twelve thousand years, plenty of time for natural selection to favor those bears carrying genes that make nutritious garbage look yummy. Grizzlies set their huge paws on the multi-millennia path to Yellowstone and Glacier National Parks' refuse when Paleo-Indians arrived to play a significant role in wiping out America's largest herbivores (and, coincidentally, predators such as saber-toothed cats that depended on them).

A kill site excavated by archeologists on the plains east of Colorado's Rocky Mountain National Park contained remains of fifteen Columbian mammoths killed 12,850 years ago, just days apart during two separate hunting events. Why a band of Paleolithic hunters would kill fifteen when merely a couple of dead mammoths would satisfy any practical needs is an anthropologic mystery likely never to be solved. But such lavish butchery eliminated all the mammoths as well as many other large plant-eating species. The kill sites also provided much grizzly bear nourishment from abandoned corpses, supplementing roots and berries.

Finally, only bison (buffalo) were left as the biggest prey left for indigenous hunters. And there were many millions of bison taking advantage of ideal grasslands in which relatively few remaining competing grazing species still roamed. Paleo-Indians intentionally widened grasslands, using fire as a tool.

After 1492, Europeans transported horses and guns across the ocean blue, eventually revolutionizing Native American life on the Great Plains and causing many farming tribes to switch to a much less trying existence as horse nomads. However, this cultural turnabout was not firmly established until a generation prior to Lewis and Clark setting out to explore along the Missouri River in 1804.

Long before horses and guns made hunting bison much more efficient, Indian hunters killed bison by driving whole herds off cliffs eroded along watercourses. Lewis and Clark's journals mention sightings of these buffalo jumps (also called *pishkums*, a Blackfeet word meaning, descriptively, "kettles of blood") on their journey of exploration along the Missouri. They also mention sightings and signs of grizzlies, which were unfamiliar to the explorers. The bears evidently fed on bison killed at buffalo jumps or that drowned when ice broke under their weight. Normally, when the expedition saw grizzlies in the vicinity of buffalo jumps, the bears were out of rifle range and quickly on their way to somewhere distant from humans.

It is true that from a good collection of Native American plains artifacts one could assemble a complete bison. All parts of the animal were used, but not all parts of every dead bison were used every time. Once you had twelve complete place settings of bison horn spoons, any more were unneeded. Thus, the bases of buffalo jumps were human garbage dumps. Hunters tried to make sure that no bison survived being driven over a cliff for fear that an escaped buffalo would warn other bison of the trap during future hunts.

A map of the historic grizzly bear range looks rather similar to an analogous map of the historic bison range. Grizzlies evolved as garbage bears over at least twelve thousand years rather than in just a century of garbage dumps in national parks. When mass hunting wiped out the wild bison herds, grizzly habitat disappeared because an important food source disappeared from the cliff bases at buffalo jumps. Grizzlies could not survive increased hunting pressure, and their range in the contiguous United States shrank to dots such as Yellowstone and Glacier National Parks.

Substituting modern human garbage for masses of abandoned mammoth bodies or masses of dead bison below buffalo jumps is a dubious solution for preserving grizzlies. Garbage consumption, although immediately beneficial to the bears, causes conflicts resulting in dead humans and, consequently, dead bears. Realizing that twelve millennia of evolution, guided by human hunting techniques, have made grizzly bears into garbage bears may help bear lovers and researchers to reduce the need for search and rescue teams to seek bear victims.

Never Before in Glacier National Park

Never before had grizzly bears killed anyone in Glacier National Park. Then within four hours one night they did—twice.

In August 1967 two nineteen-year-old women working as summer employees at national park concessions were on separate camping hikes with fellow workers when pulled from their sleeping bags by two different grizzlies. The second woman died almost at once. The first, together with a male hiking companion, was very badly injured near the tree line. Chance had assembled an amazingly skilled collection of vacationing volunteers at a remote mountain chalet within screaming distance of the bear attack. They set out with great courage on a search and rescue mission.

All the rescuers were unarmed, as guns are forbidden to be used in national parks. It's likely the search party agreed with this ban, until they had to face an always-hungry grizzly in the dark just past midnight.

A National Park Service ranger-naturalist three years older than the attack victims led the search and rescue volunteers. Hours prior to the attack, she had guided thirty-five hikers to join others at an overnight stay at the Granite Park Chalet, a little more than four miles from the Going-to-the-Sun Road through the national park. This role had fallen to her when the scheduled NPS leader was called away to fight twenty-one fires ignited by a massive lightning storm.

Among the sixty-some hikers and staff at the chalet were three physicians, all hiking separately from each other. Also present was a Native American from the Pacific Northwest with tracking experience. His hiking companion was a Catholic priest. A helicopter pilot turned out to be helpful, as did a miscellaneous cadre of strong hikers. A search and rescue team this competent would be difficult to assemble on purpose, let alone by coincidence. All that was missing was a rifle-toting marksman. He would arrive later, too late.

Most of the hikers jammed overnight in the chalet had come to see grizzly bears. The grizzlies were nightly feeders at an illegal garbage pile generated by the chalet. The chalet had an incinerator to consume its refuse, but the incinerator could not burn all the garbage the chalet created at times of peak human occupancy.

NPS personnel had warned park administrators of this danger. To the chalet staff, this bruin buffet made the bears seem like beloved pets. The staff did not fear their bear neighbors because grizzlies had never before killed anyone in Glacier.

Near the chalet were other campers who, of course, were not protected by the chalet's sturdy walls. Some were near a trailside cabin that could be climbed to quickly, and two others laid out their sleeping bags in a walk-in campground accidentally located in what turned out to be a grizzly highway. It was at the campground that a grizzly preyed on the hiking pair.

Screams from the campground had to penetrate not only the chalet's heavy walls, but also the heavy sleep of tired hikers. As it turned out, some chalet guests never woke up during the night of emergency. The campers near the trailside cabin were similarly tired but awakened quickly when a bleeding man collapsed in front of them. They gave him what aid they could and started screaming to the chalet for help.

The ranger-naturalist was unsure if there was anything to worry about, for grizzlies had never before killed anyone in Glacier. But, knowing that a bear had incited the screaming, she assembled a search party that included two of the doctors, the priest, and the Native American tracker.

The Native American, who earlier had complained to the priest about crazy white people feeding bears, announced that the only way to scare away a grizzly was with a fire. The rescuers appropriated a corrugated metal tub, added wire handles to lengthen the existing handles, and filled the tub with scrap wood. With the wood burning in the tub reflecting an inadequate glow to augment even more inadequate flashlights, the search

Grizzly bears are part of the natural fauna in Glacier, Yellowstone, and Grand Teton National Parks.

and rescue party set off down the trail to investigate the unprotected campers.

Perhaps the flaming tub worked, for the searchers did not see a bear. What they soon found, however, was bear prey, wrapped in a sleeping bag near the trailside cabin. The young man, obviously seriously hurt, maintained that his injuries were minor and that the rescuers should leave him to find the woman the grizzly had dragged away.

None of the rescuers had thought to bring a first-aid kit from the chalet because grizzlies had never before killed any human in Glacier. One of the campers at the cabin did have a well-stocked kit. He handed it to one of the doctors, who soon had the male victim ready for transport. The other doctor, a surgeon, stood close to provide further aid, if needed. The surgeon had served in Vietnam, and was schooled in the triage system of caring first for those who could be saved while leaving those likely to die to be treated later. He knew the other rescuers would find this implicit abandonment of the missing woman to be brutal.

The physician working on the mauled man called for a litter to transport him. The search and rescue team did not have a litter because grizzlies had never before killed any human in Glacier. But they quickly ripped an old frame of bedsprings off a window on the trailside cabin where the springs were supposed to substitute for bars to keep out bears. Likely a grizzly so inclined could have ripped off this frame of mattress supports with ease beyond that of the rescuers.

The mauled man kept asking about his missing hiking companion as the stretcher bearers hauled him up to the chalet. Flashlight beams grew dimmer, and in the general confusion, the party lost the trail, adding about twenty minutes to the rescue time. Once the male victim was on a chalet dining room table, the surgeon went to work.

Meanwhile, the ranger-naturalist had remained at the trailside cabin with the rest of the searchers. Although grizzlies had never before killed any human in Glacier, she had hauled a two-way radio on the search. She frantically called in the bad news to park headquarters and asked for aid, especially medical supplies, as a doctor dictated a list to her, and for a ranger with a rifle. She learned that help would arrive by helicopter in a half hour.

For all they knew, the grizzly was about to charge the rescuers from just beyond the dimming glow of fire and flashlights. The ranger-naturalist decided they would not risk further bear attack by going after the other camper while unarmed. This announcement did not meet with universal approval. Particularly in opposition were the priest and the doctor who had remained with the searchers. The Native American advised that another attack was possible. The flashlights obviously were giving out from prolonged use.

The priest was reluctant to give up but also feared to incite further deadly injury on his fellow rescuers. Tugging and straining at the fire tub, the group headed up the slope to the chalet.

At the chalet, the third doctor presented himself to the ranger-naturalist. There were now three physicians and a registered nurse to aid the mauled camper. The supplies they needed would be arriving soon by helicopter. But where would it land in the dark?

The ranger-naturalist set approximately twenty guests to preparing a landing site behind the chalet. They built fires to mark the four corners of the landing site and hauled buckets of water to prevent the fires from spreading out of control. Some grabbed axes and cut down a horse hitching rack that would threaten the helicopter's landing, while others hung lanterns on a few large stakes and pipes that were too sturdy to be removed. Then a helicopter pilot among the chalet guests came forward to guide the helicopter to the ground with instructions relayed via the ranger-naturalist's radio.

Meanwhile, a rescue party of eight or ten formed to go after the missing woman. The ranger-naturalist insisted that they wait for an armed ranger who soon would be on the ground. The alternative was for someone to fall victim to a bizarre bear acting as no grizzly had before in Glacier.

Within a few minutes, the helicopter was on the ground, and a ranger with a rifle hopped out before the rotors stopped turning. Eager hands grabbed medical supplies to haul into where the rescued camper lay. Realizing that the supplies were not sufficiently organized for immediate use, the surgeon decided the victim would be best served by a flight to a hospital. Ten or fifteen minutes after the helicopter landed, it whisked away the injured man for blood transfusion, surgery, and eventual recovery.

The newly arrived ranger ordered the ranger-naturalist to stay at the chalet to run the radio, while he led the search and rescue mission after the missing woman. As the rescuers hurried off again into the dark behind the ranger and his rifle, the third doctor joined the ranger-naturalist beside the radio and warned her that, bad as the male victim had been, the missing woman would be much worse.

As the ranger, rifle in hand, headlamp shining brightly, led the other rescuers down the hill to the site of the attack, he warned them all to stay behind him. If the bear attacked, he wanted no one in the way to frustrate his shooting. He instructed them to keep their flashlights on the bear, which would be difficult because the grizzly could move very fast. Fewer than one hundred yards along the trail, they began to step over steaming bear feces.

The Native American cut their search area in half by informing them that the bear would drag its prey downhill. They should find the spot in the campground where the attack occurred and try to follow the blood trail from there.

Having been told that noise would inform the grizzly of their approach and thus scare the bear away (which is why hikers in grizzly country wear bear bells), some of the rescuers shouted. In obvious danger, some of these had wavering voices as they cried the traditional "Whoa bear!" They searched and shouted with courage despite legitimate fear of a bear that already had attacked humans.

When they reached the campground, the attack site was obvious amid scattered gear. Blood splotched the ground both uphill *and* downhill from the attack site. The Native American tracker remembered that the male victim had said that he had run uphill. The ranger and tracker knew simultaneously that the downhill blood trail led to the woman.

Now calling the woman's name instead of "Whoa bear," the rescuers spread out to look for her despite the likely presence of a grizzly guarding its prey. The Native American spotted blood spatter on yellow glacier lily petals, and then found a bloody purse. He picked up speed downhill, and the ranger had to remind him several times to stay behind the rifle.

The searchers' flashlight batteries weakened. The tracker lost the trail. Then a weak cry brought silence to the black woods. Forgetting any fear, all the rescuers rushed toward the sound of a woman in critical trouble.

They found the nineteen-year-old in a state that seemed to defy the fact that she still was alive. Only her face remained mostly undamaged. Her lower right arm seemed to be nearly gone. As the doctor dropped to his knees beside her, everyone heard her say, "It hurts." The doctor realized that the worst injury was from puncture wounds to her chest; one lung already had collapsed.

Some rescuers turned to run up the trail about 250 yards to retrieve another set of rings from a trailside cabin window. As they left, the doctor tried to bandage the gaping wounds tightly. The woman murmured that she was cold. The doctor took off his shirt to cover her; soon she was covered by a pile of the rescuers' clothing. The doctor wondered how she had managed to live after two hours of such heavy bleeding.

While the search party sought the victim, the ranger-naturalist directed conversion of the chalet dining area into an emergency room. Tables were pulled together and covered with clean sheets. The medical supplies were sorted and organized. Plasma, intravenous needles, and morphine glinted in the yellow lights of lanterns.

About 3:30 a.m., the shouts and dimming lights of the rescue party announced their approach to the chalet. When the victim was lifted to operating table, the three doctors and nurse clustered around her, each automatically taking on a task. Faint hope evaporated as they realized how great the damage was.

They did not recognize the priest when he came forward in hiking rather than clerical garb. But they realized at once that he too was a professional with an important role to play for someone needing comfort. He spoke of God's love, and the woman seemed to relax a bit as he spoke of God's concern for her. He assured her that the doctors were working diligently to help her. He asked her if she knew that God would watch over her. She actually replied that she knew this was true.

The priest looked at the surgeon with a silent question. The surgeon replied with a very subtle shake of his head. The priest asked for water, and the nurse ran to the kitchen.

The priest asked the victim if she had been baptized. She could not speak. When he asked her if she knew that God loved her, she responded with a very slight squeeze of his hand. He said softly that he was going to use the water to trace a cross on her forehead, which would serve as a provisional baptism. As he did so, he pronounced, "I baptize you in the name of the Father, and the Son, and the Holy Spirit." He forgave her of her sins, and, to everyone's amazement, she tried to move her lips in repeating after him the words of the Act of Contrition. Then, at 4:12, she died.

Soon the helicopter returned and left with her body. Those participants in the event who still could move doused the fires around the landing pad.

When all the people still awake gathered in the chalet dining area for hot chocolate, coffee, and comfort, the ranger-naturalist announced that she was leading a mass exodus at 9:00 a.m. No one had to join the retreat, but there would be safety in numbers.

A few hours later sixty refugees, many of them former rescuers, trudged down a trail from Granite Park Chalet. Soon they would learn that another grizzly had killed another nineteen-year-old camper at another site within the national park.

On the way down, the group encountered four rangers coming up, three with rifles. Two men ran forward to beg the squad not to kill any grizzlies. It was not the bear's fault, they maintained, which was true. It was the victims' fault, they argued, which was not true. The victims had camped where directed by park regulations in a newly designated campground. No one knew the campground was where bears normally traveled near the illegal garbage dump, which had drawn the bears' two advocates as well as many others to see grizzlies at Granite Park.

The rangers passed by the protesters without comment because grizzlies had now killed humans in Glacier.

Note: Four Granite Park grizzlies eventually were killed in response to the attack. Later, a necropsy by the FBI determined that it was not human blood on the paws of one of these, the presumed killer, a mother with two cubs.

Trouble's a Bruin

In July 2003 a group of campers near Fern Lake in Colorado's Rocky Mountain National Park did everything possible to keep their camp from attracting black bears. They suspended their cooking gear and food fifteen feet above the ground from a pole installed between trees by the National Park Service. Their food was far away from their campsite, which they kept scrupulously clean.

At 7:30 a.m. one of the campers awoke with a smash to his head. Amazingly, he returned to sleep. He then was jarred from further sleep by a yet harder blow. He woke fully to blood spurting from his head, spraying all over his tent, and collecting in his lap.

Confused, he saw a black bear. He had not used a tent fly, which would have protected his tent from rain but not from a bear. (Some bear experts speculate that although a tent provides no physical protection from a bear, it might supply a psychological barrier—maybe, perhaps, sometimes.) The bear was standing outside the tent, staring eye to eye with the camper so violently awakened. The camper realized he was helpless.

The bear then wandered away toward another tent, and the camper yelled to awaken his friends. The bear repeated his wake-up call by swinging at the tent, surprisingly not tearing it. The first victim hoped that the lack of damage to the tent might indicate a lack of damage to the tent's occupant. But again, the bear walked away, and another camper crawled from his tent with blood running down his face.

The bear wandered around the campsite for a bit before meandering away. The injured campers took stock of their head wounds and emerged from a daze to realize they were in serious trouble. Their chances for

The National Park Service and the town of Estes Park cooperate in preventing black bears from raiding human food that could get the bears killed.

survival diminished as more blood poured out from both of them. They attempted to staunch the bleeding with T-shirts tied around their heads. The whole group of campers assembled on a large boulder near the lakeshore, and from this hopefully defensive position warned other hikers coming up the popular trail. About an hour later, the bear returned to slash at a food container in another campsite near Fern Lake.

A cellphone call brought two rangers tearing up the four miles from the Fern Lake Trailhead to reach the lake around 10:00 a.m. They bandaged the wounds and aided the two victims on their walk to the trailhead, a trip less easy on the descent than it had been going to Fern Lake.

Paramedics were waiting at the trailhead and conducted the battered campers to a hospital in nearby Estes Park Village. The first victim had been bitten twice in the head and had significant puncture wounds. He received twenty stitches and a rabies vaccination. The other had been carved to the skull and was clamped back together with thirty-two staples and thirty stitches.

This group of campers had done everything possible to discourage bear attack. As it happened, an oddly aggressive bear had shown up. Later, rangers killed this bear when it charged other hikers on the Fern Lake Trail. Such unusual behavior for a black bear inspired a necropsy, which revealed lesions on the bear's brain. This condition had made the bear crazy. Moreover, mayonnaise packets and aluminum foil turned up in its digestive system.

Among the many thousands of visitors who camp in Rocky Mountain National Park each year, few even see a black bear, let alone have a negative experience with one. (In 1971 there was one camper fatality near the park's western boundary by a bear accustomed to feeding on human food at a guest ranch outside the park. Subsequently, the national park acquired the ranch, of course eliminating the unnatural food source.)

The National Park Service and the Estes Park community together strive diligently to make sure the favored foods of black bears are berrylike juniper cones and kinnikinnick berries. Backcountry campers must carry commercial, hard-sided, bear-proof containers for food.

On the rare occasion when a bear turns up in a ponderosa pine in an Estes Park shopping center, it is not carrying a food bag.

AIRPLANE CRASH

Flying Franklins

———

When an airplane crashes into a mountain, it almost certainly is not where it is supposed to be. Given the nature of planes, the crash site could be just about anywhere. Therefore, searchers looking for victims and answers face a quandary about where to search. In May 2000, searchers had to perform another duty besides locating and picking up the pieces.

A husband and wife from Fort Collins, Colorado, on the plains east of Rocky Mountain National Park, were enjoying some recreation on Lake Powell, created by the damming of the Colorado River near Page, Arizona. This was a long way to go to sleep on a houseboat. But the husband had held a pilot's license for eighteen years and had accumulated more than four thousand hours of flying time. In just the past six months, he had spent fifty hours in the air, mostly back and forth to Page. A year before, he had bought a twin-engine Smith Aerostar 601 aircraft. He did not have a pilot's instrument rating amid all his experience.

On Sunday morning, April 30, the couple took off from Page to return home to Fort Collins. It had been a productive trip among the very many they had flown. Besides visiting friends and enjoying Lake Powell, they had sold their houseboat and been paid in cash.

They almost made it back to Fort Collins. Their family reported them overdue on Monday morning. They had not filed a flight plan, but they always flew the same route. This and technical data dictated a relatively narrow search area from the northern part of Rocky Mountain National Park north to Cheyenne in southern Wyoming.

The pilot had radioed the Denver Flight Service in Grand Junction, on the western edge of Colorado, at 11:15 a.m. and received a weather forecast

The summit of Comanche Peak looks over glacier-carved cliffs.

for his normal route home. He learned that there were mid- to high-level clouds with some icing conditions above the spine of the Rockies. Subsequent examination of radar data showed that the couple's plane descended to 13,300 feet about forty miles west of the 12,702-foot tall Comanche Peak on the national park's northeast boundary.

Another pilot traveling the same route about fifteen minutes behind the Fort Collins couple later reported that the sky was overcast, with clouds two hundred feet below the altitude of Comanche. This pilot swung north to the vicinity of Cheyenne in order to see where he was flying.

The couple's unwitnessed crash later was deemed to be due to pilot error of descending too soon in an area of poor visibility. Had he been a hundred feet higher, the pilot would have cleared the last mountain barrier before home. It was not known if ice buildup on his wings reduced his ability to lift the plane to a safe altitude.

May is not a lovely month at 12,700 feet, and blowing snow and clouds often block visibility at this altitude. It wasn't until May 4 that the crew of a Colorado National Guard helicopter were able to spot the wreckage, a short way within the national park boundary. The plane had hit the mountain slope at a low angle, perhaps trying to gain altitude. Wreckage scattered over approximately two acres, some falling over the ridge to outside the national park.

The day after the discovery, two National Park Service rangers, a Larimer County coroner, and a National Transportation Safety Board investigator helicoptered to the crash site. They collected what identifiable body parts they could. The remains of the aircraft were removed August 6. Snow cover and the low angle of impact had protected the alpine tundra from significant damage.

The initial on-site investigators on May 5 also noticed $100 bills billowing around the crash site. They were able to collect more than $7,000 from the houseboat sale to deliver to the heirs. This obviously was a substantial sum, but likely some of the Federal Reserve notes escaped recovery.

The high winds that delayed finding the crash site had five days to scatter currency over a broad area with no woody plant tall enough to snag it. Some perhaps were blown out of sight beneath rocks. Perhaps some were collected by pikas, cute round-eared rabbit relatives that are active at high altitudes throughout the year.

The crash on the relatively gentle west slope by which climbers reach the summit of Comanche sent pieces of the plane over cliff edges that form bowls of glacier-carved cirques on the east-facing side of the peak. The fierce winds from the west that frustrated the searchers had been characteristic of the peak for many millennia. In ages of more snowfall than in the relatively warm present, this wind had picked up tons of snow to drop on the east side of Comanche, eventually forming glaciers, rivers of ice that carved the dramatic cliffs on the east side and left behind Emmaline and Cirque Lakes far below, together with many unnamed pools.

Likely this same wind carried an unknowable number of $100 bills to dump on the cliffs, in the lakes, or in the subalpine forest watered by melting snow.

The $100 bills used for the houseboat payment might have been of three different designs printed with ever-increasing complexity to foil counterfeiters. The paper and ink used were distinctive and expected to last for fifteen years of use as money. Of course, $100 bills are exchanged less often than fives or twenties. Hundreds, with their portrait of Ben Franklin, would last longer in a desk drawer or in a pika den.

The Bureau of Engraving and Printing will redeem mutilated currency forever, if Treasury Department experts are satisfied that missing remnants have been destroyed. Even the sturdiest paper has many enemies, such as water, fire, insects, rodents, or pikas. Every year the Treasury processes approximately thirty thousand claims of mutilated currency totaling more than $30 million.

Of course, any $100 bills dislodged by wind from under rocks, or by gravity from cirque walls, or by evaporation from lakes, or by red squirrels from spruce branches, when found by hikers should be turned over to the National Park Service for delivery to the heirs of the plane crash victims. Such is the morality-lifting experience of mountain environments.

Tribesman II

In 1950 a band of missionaries accepted the risk of martyrdom pierced by arrows in South America's equatorial jungles. They did not, however, expect mass martyrdom on a snowbound cliff high in Grand Teton National Park.

In 1942 the New Tribes Mission had assembled 450 nonsectarian Protestants dedicated to "reaching new tribes until we've reached the last one." In June 1950 the mission's first airplane, called *Tribesman*, crashed in Venezuela, killing fifteen missionaries. In November of that year, many surviving family members (ten adults, three crew, and eight children, two only six months old) were on *Tribesman II*, determined to carry on with the efforts of their martyred loved ones. They were headed to Montana for a religious rally before flying to Bolivia to undertake conversion of previously unknown tribes.

On the way to Montana, *Tribesman II* encountered clouds hiding 12,549-foot Mount Moran in Wyoming's Grand Teton National Park. At 4:40 p.m. the twin-engine C-47 clipped a wing on a huge rock and crashed into a northeast ridge above Skillet Glacier, about one thousand feet below the summit.

A bright explosion briefly pinpointed the crash site viewed from below. The temperature was falling rapidly. A blizzard was forecast for the next day, and the picturesque Mount Moran had not yet been climbed in winter. Yet, the park's chief ranger knew that a search and rescue team would have to try to ascend to the crash site in the near hopeless chance that someone on the plane had survived.

Mount Moran and Skillet Glacier reflect in Oxbow Bend, home to white pelicans.

Four climbing rangers started up, carrying only first-aid supplies and survival gear. Backing them up were five pararescuemen ready to drop onto Moran, if they could help. Unfortunately, a roaring blizzard forced the climbers to retreat.

Two local climbing guides experienced in the Tetons set out on a second attempt. With three Air Service rescuemen to man a radio relay camp halfway up, they began climbing.

Near sunset two days after the crash, a search plane spotted the wreckage far from where the climbers were directing their ascent. The relay radio, however, failed to work. At 1:00 a.m. three rangers set off on cross-country skis through unbroken, waist-deep snow to catch up with the climbers. After they managed to overtake the climbers to inform them of their misdirection, the advance team of guides undertook a dangerous traverse to the crash site.

On November 25, hammering pitons (metal spikes driven into cracks in the rock to support a climber or a rope) to secure their route across especially icy cliffs, the two climbers reached scattered remnants of the large aircraft. They were unsurprised to discover that no one had survived. After ninety minutes of searching, note-taking, and photo documentation, the two climbers descended from an expectedly fruitless rescue, having found only one charred body.

The climbers' expert advice was that the National Park Service should not undertake any further hazardous investigation of the site in winter. Moreover, the Civil Aeronautics Board requested that climbing Mount Moran in the vicinity of the crash site should be prohibited until the board could complete its investigation. The northeast ridge was closed for five years.

In mid-July after the crash, a local climbing guide and an NPS ranger joined forces to check the crash site. They found it still covered by eight to ten feet of snow. The following month, after considerable melting, three climbing guides shepherded a relatively large group of investigators to the crash. Two NPS rangers searched for personal effects that were scattered in cracks and crevices all over the precipice, and they gathered body parts. Two physicians tried to identify the remains. A minister representing New

Tribes Mission, whose wife had died in the first mission crash, made the climb and conducted a service over a large crack in the mountain where the remains were interred. Three Wyoming investigators represented the state, and a single reporter provided press coverage. Absent snow and ice, the guides kept everyone safe.

Four victims were blown to no one knew where. The airplane's tail remained in place, a weathered memorial above the distinctive Skillet Glacier to the missionaries and their families. In subsequent years these martyrs were followed by other New Tribes missionaries killed by Communist guerillas in Colombia and the Philippines. Between 1950 and 1952, various awards were bestowed on the climbers who ventured up a hopeless search and rescue route.

SLIDE

Neurosurgery at Chasm Lake

Lambs Slide is a permanent snowfield that defines the base of the vertical wall of the East Face on Longs Peak in Colorado's Rocky Mountain National Park. The snowfield gained its name when, in 1871, preacher, pioneer, and hotel keeper Elkanah Lamb slipped at the top of the snowfield. He bypassed exposed rocks while sliding down to slow in the less steep grade near the bottom. Throwing his arm around another projecting rock, he broke a pocketknife blade chipping a toehold in the ice-cemented snow and inched his way to safety unhurt.

It may be that this divine protection of Reverend Lamb was repeated in January 1968. Another accidental slider failed to miss the rocks. But there were mountaineering physicians below the East Face on a frigid night to perform successful neurosurgery in a dark, stone shelter cabin.

Jim Disney, experienced mountaineer and talented painter of admirable landscapes, led three companions up the Longs Peak Trail at 3:00 a.m. to climb the East Face to the 14,259-foot summit. It was a normal starting time for this popular climbing destination, but January was a daunting month to attempt an ascent. They kicked and hoped to glide on cross-country skis, ascending through thin, cold air amid thickly growing lodgepole pines. At dim sunrise about 6:00 a.m., they carried their skis above the trees across alpine tundra where wind scoured away the snow. Where there were few rocks on which to trip, the tundra was frozen hard as the rocks. In scattered sheltered stretches, they snapped their boots back into the ski bindings.

The winter climb was tough enough to be newsworthy. The group carried two handheld radios borrowed from the National Park Service. They planned to participate in a live broadcast on the NBC monitor from New York City via radio station KLOV in the town of Loveland, Colorado. What made the climb of particular interest was its route up the 1,800-foot East Face, which had a grim history of fatality.

The selected route, called Kiener's Route, was the least difficult way up the East Face. This was the route of the first winter ascent of the East Face in 1925 by Walter Kiener and Agnes Vaille, which resulted in Vaille's death from hypothermia.

The 1968 plan was to divide the climb into two days, bivouacking on a ledge ironically called Broadway above Lambs Slide and below the vertical ascent of the East Face. The four climbers ascended Lambs Slide using crampons (a hinged assemblage of spikes attached by straps to boot soles) and ice axes. To save time during the short winter days, they were not roped together. Fatigue, poor weather, and equipment problems delayed the group, which was still ascending Lambs Slide around 8:30 p.m., long after dark.

Wisely, they decided to retreat to a stone shelter cabin below Chasm Lake at the base of the East Face before continuing to the summit the next day. As they started back down Lambs Slide, a hinge on a crampon worn by group member Dick Kezlan broke. Kezlan, however, was unaware of his equipment failure. When he tried to jam the crampon into the icy snow in the usual fashion, it caused his foot to turn and flipped him face first into the hard-packed snow. Perhaps the impact stunned him, because although practiced in arresting such a fall, he just groaned and slid past his companions, who were shouting in vain for him to dig in with his ice axe. Then they heard a crunch, which had not echoed from surrounding cliffs when Elkanah Lamb made his more fortunate slide.

Descending to Kezlan's unconscious form in the snow, his companions discovered that his head was laid open and his face was masked by blood. It was dark, and the wind chill was the equivalent of twenty degrees below zero. At least they had radios to notify the National Park Service about the injury and the deteriorating weather.

Within minutes, rangers and two rescue groups, including doctor Sam Luce, veteran of many search and rescue missions, and ranger Bob Haines

Lambs Slide slants below the East Face of Longs Peak.

were on their way. Just as the need for search and rescue often comes when victims are tired, search and rescue team members often do not respond to the emergency after a restful day lying around waiting for something awful to happen.

Thus it was that Sam Luce had just returned home after a long day treating patients when the phone call cancelled any hope for a hot dinner and restful evening. Hearing the initial description of the accident, he filled a pack with forty pounds of medical gear and ran out to a ride with rangers headed for the Longs Peak Trailhead. Within an hour of the fall and slide, they were on the trail. They forced their way into a fifty-mile-per-hour gale slamming snow into their faces for eight miles to Lambs Slide. It took them four hours of brutal hiking, a praiseworthy effort in a dark blizzard.

Meanwhile, Jim Disney left two companions with the unconscious Kezlan to descend across a slope of loose rock to the west side of frozen Chasm Lake and slip-and-slide his way to the east shore. He then climbed down a fairly short but steep rock slab to the stone shelter cabin sitting in an alpine meadow about a mile from the crash on Lambs Slide. He hoped that the cabin might contain blankets or more first-aid supplies.

He found instead that it contained two men in sleeping bags. One was Dee Crouch, an internist from Denver's Colorado General Hospital, who was intending to ascend the East Face with his companion the next day. The two climbers emerged from their bags, pulled on their clothes, and headed with Disney across Chasm Lake.

Kneeling beside Kezlan, the internist was surrounded by a jumble of scattered mountaineering gear, ropes, and blood-stained snow. He could see in the flashlights' beams what needed to be done, but he had no means at hand to do it. Tools such as a scalpel and forceps normally are not necessary for climbing Longs and were not sliding around in the unsterile bottom of his pack. All he could do was try to keep the victim warm until medical supplies arrived.

Dr. Luce and his ranger team arrived sweating in temperatures well below zero. Nearly hypothermic themselves by this time, they and the other climbers decided to retreat to the Chasm Lake shelter while the two doctors and the rescuers struggled to maintain Kezlan's life. First, Dr. Luce removed intravenous fluid from his pack (contained in glass bottles in 1968) as well as drugs to reduce swelling in the victim's brain and halt convulsions. The first challenge was finding a vein through which to administer the intravenous medications. This was a near-superhuman task in the dark, cold, and wind. In addition, the bitter cold froze the fluids in their containers and the IV tubes. At times Luce had to resort to using a syringe to slowly administer the fluids that he thawed by keeping the frigid bottles under his coat next to his skin.

About an hour before dawn, more rangers and rescue teams arrived with a litter to carry Kezlan to the stone shelter cabin a mile of rolling rock and slick ice away. The cabin was tiny for the rescue teams and victim, but at least the stone walls diminished the wind. Flashlights focused on Kezlan's head, and his litter sat between two footlockers. Disney managed the light, and the two doctors reassessed the damage.

After cleaning away blood clots, they could see that the victim's condition was unsurprisingly horrible. His skull had three major fractures, one in his right temple impinging on his brain, one from his right ear to his right eye, and one around the base of his skull. He was bleeding from several severe cuts.

First the doctors stopped the bleeding. Then Luce began sterilizing surgical instruments, including a cooking spoon, over the flame of a gas camping stove. He opened Kezlan's skull to relieve pressure on the brain, and a cup of jellylike blood oozed from the incision, relieving the pressure. Kezlan became semiconscious. Luce used forceps to lift a bone fragment back in place to close the wound.

It took only three hours for rescuers to lower and haul Kezlan's litter from Chasm Lake to an ambulance for the ride to the hospital and eventual recovery. Thirty-seven rescuers had gotten Kezlan out alive. Dr. Luce suffered slight frostbite (slight hurts more than slightly) to his toes by crouching by the victim in the early morning subzero dark while waiting for the litter to arrive. Later, he was called upon to lecture how neurosurgery in a dark, jammed, cold cabin at 11,600 feet could save a life.

All the rescuers likely had their stories to tell about this achievement. Ranger Bob Haines, who accompanied Luce, was rugged enough to always add a bulky twin-lens reflex camera to his large pack of ranger gear. His talks about his park explorations and adventures, illustrated by two-and-a-quarter-inch square photographic slides, were highly regarded in the Estes Park community.

Perhaps none were more fascinating than his account of the rescue of Dick Kezlan. Haines did not show photographs of the grim surgery that took place, but he did show a picture taken inside the crowded stone hut where food was being heated over a gas cookstove, perhaps the same stove that had sterilized the surgical tools.

The photo showed a bedraggled, cold rescuer heating a pot of food. From his red nose, an eighteen-inch straight line of white mucous descended unnoticed into the pot. In the near darkness with eyes tearing from the wind, it is certain that no one, including Haines, saw this element of grim humor. The light that flashed a tiny fraction of a second could have shown it only to the film.

Very likely Haines did not notice this sign of search and rescue stress and weariness, glamour and glory, until days later when he viewed the processed slide. But he delighted in pointing it out to his lecture audiences.

There's the Ranger Now

When a ranger hears the words "There's the ranger now" amid a group of wilderness visitors, good news is unlikely. So it was in 1906 or 1907, when US Forest Service ranger Frank Liebig was on patrol in what would become Glacier National Park. He had ridden horseback from east to west over the Continental Divide at Gunsight Pass to Sperry Glacier late in the summer day.

What was then part of a "forest reserve" attracted tourists, some of whom ran over to the ranger to report that a woman had slipped and fallen into a crevasse, or crack, in glacial ice. They did not know how to rescue her.

Liebig evidently formed a plan at once. He used his axe to cut a stunted five-inch-thick fir about five feet long growing at the tree line. He then took ropes that had lashed gear to two pack horses and called for the tourists to follow him about a quarter mile to the edge of the glacier. They crossed about two hundred yards of ice to look over the edge of the crevasse, where several more men peered into where the woman had fallen.

Liebig chopped a hole in the ice on the lower edge of the crevasse, stuck the fir trunk in, and packed ice around it to hopefully hold the trunk in place. He tied his two lash ropes together, tied knots along the line to aid in climbing, and tied the line to the fir post. He told two men to hang onto the post to keep it from pulling out of the hole with his weight.

Looking down the crevasse, which was about four or five feet wide at the top, he could see the woman some thirty feet below, wedged where the crack narrowed. She was horizontal and apparently dead. He threw the end of the rope down and began to descend knot to knot. It was sweaty work until he reached the woman, where he was thoroughly chilled by the surrounding ice.

He tried to hang onto the rope with one hand and pull the victim loose with the other, but she was wedged in too tightly to budge. The surrounding ice walls were smooth and slick, offering no place to get a foothold. All he could do was stand on her wedged body and send the rope up for the axe to be lowered to him. This accomplished, he chopped footholds on each side of the crevasse, and sent his axe up again on the rope.

When the rope again descended, he set his feet in the newly chopped steps and pulled on one of the woman's arms, but she was wedged so tightly he feared he would dislocate it. Finally, though, he did manage to dislodge her and tied the rope around her waist, whereupon the men at the top pulled her out. By this time the ranger was so thoroughly frozen he could not climb back up the knotted rope. He fastened the rope under his arms, and the team on top pulled him up. Once out of the ice crack, he was able to exercise to increase blood circulation and warm himself.

More rescuers arrived with a lantern and candles to offset the near darkness. However, there was no stretcher available. Four men lifted the woman's body, one on each arm and leg, and carried her to the glacier's edge. From there a faint trail led down a slope of rock previously deposited by the moving ice and around some cliffs. One of these was more than twenty feet high. Here the rescuers decided that the safest procedure was to lower the woman's body down the cliff after some of the party went ahead on the narrow trail to receive her.

When her body was about halfway down, it began to rotate, banging her head on the rocks, opening a gash. Evidently, this collision caused her to regain consciousness, and she screamed in pain. This thoroughly startled the rescuers, who all had assumed she was dead. She then fainted again.

At last, they carried her to a camp below the tree line, where there was fuel for a large fire. Eager hands brewed coffee and heated brandy, and everyone warmed themselves with the hot drinks. The body bearers and the ranger collapsed into sleeping bags, worn out from exertion (with some also feeling the effects of the brandy).

Jackson Glacier is one of the surviving glaciers in Glacier National Park, where global warming is predicted to melt all of them by 2030.

Other rescuers managed to warm the victim and revive her, filling her also with brandy until she became intoxicated. Likely this first-aid procedure was of dubious merit.

Early the next morning, a physician arrived on the scene and determined that the woman was unharmed. Given that she had fallen thirty feet to freeze while unconscious in a crevasse, been forcefully dislodged from the ice, hauled without a litter, had a gash scoured in her scalp, and needed to recover from a drunken stupor, the doctor's opinion also might have been of dubious merit.

But she recovered. She would have died had she remained within the glacier overnight.

Today, the risk of freezing on Sperry Glacier has been much reduced by global warming, which has melted the bulk of the ice to flow down ominously named Avalanche Creek. By 2030 all the glaciers of Glacier National Park likely will be merely an old story of search and rescue.

DROWN

Venturi Speed

In Colorado's Rocky Mountain National Park, the Big Thompson River meanders peacefully through the glacier-leveled expanse of Moraine Park. At the eastern end of the South Lateral Moraine ridge, however, the terrain steepens. Here also the river flows over remnants of a terminal moraine, large boulders dropped millennia ago at the farthest end of a glacial ice sheet. The river's character changes from gentle to fierce.

Forced by the boulders to flow through constricted space, the river must race among them at a faster speed in order to maintain the same amount of flow as above this choke point. The need for water to increase speed as gravity forces the same volume of fluid through a narrower space is called the Venturi effect, named for Giovanni Venturi, an Italian physicist born in the eighteenth century who first described the phenomenon. In 2001, this increased water speed drowned a nine-year-old boy where the Big Thompson River switched from placid to deadly.

A substantial bridge carries Bear Lake Road across this whitewater torrent that rushes over boulders rounded by glacial milling and slickened by melted snow and invisible patches of algae. At the bridge's north end, small parking areas allow motorists to pause and exit their cars to look closely at the impressive drama of water splashing noisily amid spray-covered rocks. This wonder is a delight, particularly for small children.

The melted snow gushed with maximum spectacle that May, when father, mother, and their nine-year-old son drove up from the plains to

Opposite: The Big Thompson River swollen by melting snow crashes amid boulders next to a bridge.

visit the national park. The sky was blue, and the temperature was what passed for warm at eight thousand feet above sea level. A fine mist cooled the air a bit alongside the crashing Big Thompson River. It justified the park's reputation as summer heaven.

Anglers pursued catch-and-release recreation with the river's trout. The river practiced catch but not release when father and son sought an even better view on a bankside boulder as the mother relaxed on a dry rock nearby.

Amid the water racket, the father turned momentarily to gaze at the view upstream. The boy shifted a bit to see what his dad saw. Suddenly, his feet slipped, and he plunged silently into the noisy stream, invisible in an instant when his father turned back to where his son had been.

The water was cold but not so cold that it hurt the boy. The green lichen crust on the rock had looked dry, not slick. What had hap—?

The roaring river pulled him down. He could touch nothing solid. The water slammed him under a rounded lip of a boulder. His head hit rock. He never knew the invincible torrent held him hidden under the boulder, under the water.

At 1:50 p.m. the park headquarters received word of a child missing at the Big Thompson River bridge. A quick search by rangers downstream did not discover the missing boy. Soon further help came from the Estes Park Volunteer Fire Department and its dive team, the Larimer County Sheriff's dive team, and scent search dogs. Within an hour more than fifty searchers walked both sides of the river and probed pools near the place where the child had disappeared.

All of the searchers hoped the child would be on land downstream. All hoped that they would fail to discover a small body in the water. One team failed to fail.

After nearly three hours of searching, a team found the boy's body in a deep pool not far from where he had slipped from the boulder. A dive team went to work. They could not retrieve the morning's bright joy and hope lost in an instant.

The National Park Service posted conspicuous signs next to the river, proclaiming "Danger: Swift Water. Stay back from riverbanks and the river: boulders are treacherously slick. If you fall in, icy water will quickly incapacitate you and swift currents can kill you." The lower half of the sign is an obvious silhouette of a child falling into a rushing stream.

Presumably, parents understand the meaning of the long word *incapacitate* and can shout a translation to kids. Parents are surely more inclined to heed the signs than is a small child intent on unfamiliar rushing water, temporarily deaf to parental commands, and drawn to appealing natural playground boulders slick from a thin layer of invisible algae and from whitewater pushed at Venturi speed.

Deep and Cold

———————

Montana's Glacier National Park is named for frozen water. Even in its liquid form, all of Glacier's water was recently ice. Streams and lakes are never warmer than fifty degrees Fahrenheit at the surface.

Thus, when a six-year-old boy from Seattle slipped into McDonald Creek near his father below a turnout on Going-to-the-Sun Road, his body chilled quickly to immobility. Rushing melted ice grabbed him out of sight except for brief unseen exposure as the body plunged over Upper and Lower McDonald Falls. It was 6:00 p.m.

Propelled by parental fear, the father plunged into the water in pursuit of his son, only to be immersed. The creek's frigid temperature informed the father of the futility of his rescue efforts. He fought his way back to shore, where his other two sons waited for him. They ran back to their car to drive for help.

When they encountered a National Park Service ranger, search and rescue teams rushed immediately into action. A ranger happened to be teaching a first-aid class at park headquarters near the park's west entrance, and the class of thirty immediately divided into two groups to join NPS searchers along McDonald Creek some fourteen miles north.

Also quickly on the scene were members of the Flathead County Search and Rescue unit, including twelve scuba divers. Seven searched in McDonald Creek; five dove in Lake McDonald near the creek's mouth. Lake McDonald is 10 miles long (the longest lake in the park), 1.5 miles wide, and 440 feet deep. The boy's body was drifting toward this deepest, coldest lake in Glacier. Two experienced volunteers teamed to search a series of ledges in the less-deep creek.

Lake McDonald is the deepest and longest lake in Glacier National Park.

At 4:00 a.m. the next day, the pair began searching a deep part of the lake beyond the delta at the creek's mouth. Here they were blasted unexpectedly by a strong current sweeping from its plunge over McDonald Falls. The force of the current amounted to a waterfall beneath the lake's surface.

Rising from an approximate depth of 60 feet where their aqualung tanks had run low, the pair encountered an underwater cascade that pushed them down to about 140 feet. They attempted to hold on to each other, but the current's force broke them apart. One diver managed to reach the surface near the creek's mouth. Other rescuers waited to see his partner's yellow tank rising through the water. After several painfully long minutes, they admitted that their missing search team member had drowned.

The surviving diver had risen from the water so quickly that he was in danger from the bends. This medical condition, which is very painful and frequently fatal, is caused by nitrogen bubbles coming out of solution in various parts of the body due to the rapid lowering of pressure from deep beneath the water. When the diver rose too quickly for his body to expel the bubbles naturally, they could have blocked his blood vessels.

The diver was saved by flying him in an airplane internally pressurized to a high level to a decompression chamber at Brownlee Dam in Idaho. Under careful supervision, he spent thirty-eight hours in the chamber until his body pressure dropped to normal.

One drowned diver and a near miss for his partner set off an alarm for the searchers. The park's chief ranger decided that the six-year-old's body was beyond recovery, having likely come to rest somewhere in the lake. The search was repurposed to finding the body of the drowned diver, who had been lost at a known location.

The remaining divers obtained larger tanks and used safety lines to eliminate further loss of life. About twenty-four hours after the initial slip and fall of the boy, the diver who had attempted to find him was himself found by two of his teammates about a hundred feet below the lake's surface.

The search for the boy's body continued in anticipation that it would rise to the surface within a few days. It did not. Searchers began to wonder if the body might still be jammed somewhere in the creek, though they thought it unlikely.

For the next several weeks, rangers searched twice daily near the creek mouth for the missing child. They used a grappling hook to try to snag the corpse. When efforts seemed futile, checks were reduced to every few days. It seemed as though the body would never be found.

After almost two months, a park resident reported seeing a white shoe jammed between boulders about four feet deep in the lake, approximately a mile from where the boy originally had fallen. The victim still was wearing the shoe. The accidental location of a missing body is a fairly common occurrence after extensive search and rescue efforts have failed.

Flash Flood

Survivors of the Big Thompson Canyon Flood universally comment on three things: July 31, 1976, was a mostly delightful, blue-sky day. Clouds that assembled in the late afternoon were not gray, but black, necessitating driving with headlights. And the stench of propane escaping from countless burst tanks sent floating down the river by the flood was horrid.

Extremely common comments from survivors express great sorrow for loss of family, friends, pets, and property as well as great gratitude to God for rescue when 144 died in Colorado's greatest natural disaster. Survivors' regard for life increased along with determination to use life for good.

Unusual winds from the south brought Pacific moisture in air that mostly avoided the Sierra Nevada and Wasatch mountains, which normally elevate air from the Pacific to higher altitude, draining much of its moisture. Additional soggy air arrived from the Gulf of Mexico and Caribbean with no mountain barrier. Cold air descended from Canada, reducing the amount of water the atmosphere could hold.

The three winds converged in a rare confluence near 13,560-foot Hagues Peak, third highest in Rocky Mountain National Park. Forced at last to cold, higher altitude, the water-laden air rose to sixty thousand feet in massive thunderheads that darkened the sky and blocked out the sun. Pushed from three directions, torrents of rain stalled above the middle of the Big Thompson River drainage and dumped four inches of rain an hour on solid rock that absorbed nothing.

Within four hours, a twenty-foot-high wall of water funneled at fourteen miles per hour and one thousand cubic feet per second onto residents of a twenty-five-mile-long, vertical-walled canyon and a mass of motorists on US Highway 34 attracted to the scenic glory of the canyon and of Rocky Mountain National Park, a short way to the west. Even when the warnings came to stay out or get out of the canyon, many soon-to-be victims were experiencing little or no rain at their locations.

The floodwall ripped centuries-old ponderosa pines out by their roots and swept huge boulders to grind together in the river along with most houses, recreational vehicles, trailers, and tents along the riverbanks to twenty feet above the canyon floor. Vehicles with canyon residents and masses of tourists inside bobbed in the flood, headlights glowing from under the water while passengers screamed mostly unheard for help. Eventually around 430 crushed vehicles were recovered, some swept empty from canyon residences, some abandoned by those lucky enough or perceptive enough to climb, and some still containing drowned passengers. Statistics indicate that two-thirds of drowning victims in flash floods perish in cars trying to escape.

From about halfway into the canyon, an amateur radio operator called the first warning of water on the road. Other reports announced rockslides, which caused the Colorado State Patrol to contact one of their sergeants, off-duty and watching television with his wife, to head up the canyon to investigate.

The sergeant left home at once and raced up Highway 34 to find the flood. At 8:45 p.m., he began using a bullhorn to warn residents to get out of their homes and climb. At 9:00 p.m., he radioed to the State Patrol that people alongside the river and anyone working at the power plant in the canyon should get out. At 9:15, he radioed that his car was in the middle of the flood and he could not get out, and that everyone downstream should evacuate. He did not answer further calls. Eventually, his body was found around eight miles downstream from his final radio call site. His car was crushed beyond recognition and was identified only by its Colorado State Patrol key ring.

Other state patrolmen dodged washouts and rockslides to warn canyon residents to flee. At 8:35 p.m., one radioed his location about seven and a half miles into the canyon. There, a thirty-foot wall of water that washed from a side gully smashed into his car and flung it into the river. He managed to radio a warning to "start taking people out" and next shouted, "The whole mountainside is gone!" Swimming miraculously to safety, he joined

Larimer County Sheriff's Department officers to clear campgrounds and houses of potential victims.

Another state trooper set up a roadblock to prevent motorists from driving into the canyon. The angry travelers eventually numbered seventy-five, some arguing that they had to get to a motel where they had reservations. That motel was obliterated. All the guests at a nearby motel were drowned, and the only sign of the lodging was a register eventually found in the water hundreds of miles away near the Kansas border.

A temporary police officer hired by the town of Estes Park to help deal with the seasonal summer crush was off-duty, driving up the canyon with his pregnant wife. When he saw the rising water and falling boulders, he stopped to send her climbing the canyon wall and then raced through the canyon, warning at least sixty people to flee the flood. He tried to climb a utility pole, the only hope nearby when the water wall hit. The pole snapped, sending another hero to drown.

The law enforcement agencies were overwhelmed trying to cope with losing officers and dealing with a massive disaster. At 9:45 p.m., fifty-five staff from Rocky Mountain National Park waded into the fray with heavy equipment operators led by the park's maintenance chief and search and rescue rangers led by the park's chief ranger.

Of course, the National Park Service initially concentrated search and rescue efforts at the west end of the canyon, which was nearest them. A short way into the canyon, the rescue crews encountered high water and the highway washed out from side gullies gushing torrents into the river. Heavy equipment operators carved a way through the debris for search and rescue teams to follow with care.

Flood and debris barred them only three miles from the open Estes Valley. At a bend in the river, they found thirty to forty stranded people. Relentless rain nearly blinded NPS searchers in the dark, but they assembled a rescue convoy back up the canyon by 1:00 a.m. Soon they discovered that they were all

Opposite: A United States Geological Survey geologist explains how a rushing river can use a rock to scour a U-shaped trench in a boulder along the Big Thompson Canyon.

trapped by high water. Rangers scaled steep, wet terrain to install ropes should water rise further to force a climb to safety, which, thankfully, did not happen.

By 3:00 a.m. the rain seemed to diminish, and the chief ranger led another attempt to escape with his charges up the canyon toward Estes Park. A few private vehicles were in the line. Another rush of water from a cross-gully stopped the convoy, but a husband and wife in a heavy, four-wheel-drive pickup swung around the rangers to buck though the torrent. It dumped the truck upside down in the middle of the river. Despite repeated ranger rescue efforts amid strobe-like lightning flashes, the couple drowned as the smell of ozone from constant lightning strikes filled the night air.

By dawn around 5:30, most NPS personnel had retreated from the canyon with their rescued victims. The rescue teams changed out of uniforms soaked with cold water and caked with mud. By 7:00 p.m. they were back in the canyon, forcing a primitive road through to search for and rescue more victims and grimly aid in the recovery of 139 bodies. Five ultimately remained buried, never found under tons of rock and sediment.

The rangers also helped set up helicopter landing areas, but continued rain grounded choppers the day after the flood. Volunteers assembled four-wheel-drive vehicles and horses to traverse little-known, rugged routes into the canyon to extract victims. They noticed dense flocks of broad-tailed hummingbirds whose feeders had been carried away along with human residences. Helicopters could fly the next day and airlifted 850 people to safety.

For two weeks the National Park Service continued to aid post-flood recovery. Bodies were found. Rangers helped block sightseers and looters, and park maintenance crews joined volunteers from across America in road construction and wreckage removal. Less heroic tasks included providing water and port-a-potties for residents remaining above flood level and for recovery and reconstruction teams.

For their unselfish heroism and skill during the flood, national park staff received the State of Colorado Governor's Citation and Department of Interior Unit Valor Award. There were many awards to be handed out from various agencies and organizations and many stories to be written by survivors of the Big Thompson Canyon Flood.

AVALANCHE

Cornice Collapse

Cornices are overhanging layers of snow that are formed when wind picks up clouds of snow and deposits it along the ridgeline of a mountain. Heavy, wet snow piling up quickly at the edge of a drop also can form a cornice until its weight becomes too heavy for the mass to continue to defy gravity.

Cornice snow clings to itself but is unsupported below. It can form on roofs or on the edges of broad expanses of mountain summits. Cornice collapse from either can be fatal to people unlucky enough to be beneath the falling masses of snow.

Prevailing winds from the west across the aptly named 12,324-foot Flattop Mountain in Colorado's Rocky Mountain National Park have dumped snow for many millennia. When enough snow thus has been deposited (more than melts in summer), glaciers eventually form into ice rivers. Glaciers flow downhill, carving cliffs and gullies on the east flanks below the flat summit that offers no barrier to wind. Tyndall Glacier, named for the British physicist and mountaineer who described the mechanics of global warming in the nineteenth century, still hangs on the southeast flank of Flattop.

On the northeast flank of Flattop, ice walls also form in winter but are not large enough to remain through most summers and eventually expand to glaciers. They do, however, form playgrounds for mountaineers to practice ice climbing.

In November 1992 two ice climbers (one a professional climbing guide) were ascending in a gully (also called a couloir) on the northeast side of Flattop. Two female companions of the climbers patiently watched them climb from the bottom of the couloir. The women later reported that

When wind picks up clouds of snow to drop atop cliff edges, it can form unstable ledges called cornices.

around 1:00 p.m. a large gust of wind caused blowing snow to hide their view up to the climbers for several minutes.

When the snow died down and their view cleared, they no longer could see the climbers, and there was a large buildup of snow at the bottom of the gully. Moreover, the wind had seemed to arise and disappear suddenly on a rare winter day that otherwise seemed relatively calm.

It's possible that the women were not experienced enough to know that these events signaled an extremely bad accident. Or perhaps they already suspected that the conditions they had witnessed likely were fatal to the climbers. In either case, they returned to their camp on a relatively level stretch of the Odessa Lake Trail to wait.

As darkness approached, the women hiked back down to a road at Bear Lake to notify friends in the climbing community and the National Park

Service rangers. Rangers headed up the Odessa Lake Trail that evening to the campsite, where they built a fire and lit lanterns in hopes of leading the climbers back to camp. This failed to work.

The weather deteriorated the following morning, but searchers covered the area at the base of the couloir. By the second morning after the climbers had disappeared, searchers climbed Flattop and looked down its north ridge, despite forty-mile-per-hour wind masking everything with blowing snow and misery. These searchers spotted the missing men's ice axes and packs, which were just sitting on a rock, undamaged, as though they had been placed there to be retrieved soon.

The searchers also noticed that a cornice at the top of the couloir recently had broken away and had not yet been restored by the howling wind. Likely this cornice had fallen due to temporary warming or too much added weight from more windblown snow. This had been an avalanche that rushed down on the climbers on the vertical ice. The falling snow mass displaced the air that had created the temporary wind gust and cloud of snow the two women had seen before their climbing companions disappeared.

The weather grew ever more hostile as the searchers continued probing the avalanche snow chunks at the bottom of the couloirs. By the fourth day, the wind was setting up more deadly avalanche potential above the searchers. The search obviously could not end well and was terminated.

The snowfall in the winter of 1992–93 was far beyond normal. This was a happy circumstance for the moisture-deprived communities east of the Rockies, but it made body recovery impossible. The snow did not melt sufficiently for the National Park Service or professional mountain guides to find the ice climbers' bodies in the summer of 1993 or most of the summer of 1994. Finally, though, in August of 1994, one of the bodies melted out. Two weeks later searchers found the second body.

Predicting this tragedy would have been difficult, even for the highly experienced and competent winter climbers involved. Slightly moderating weather in late autumn perhaps destabilized cornices. But early winter was not a prime time for cornice collapse.

If avalanche beacons had been carried by all four members of the original group, they might have led the two women to dig out the buried men. These beacons are battery-powered devices that transmit a radio signal which can lead searchers with similar devices to victims buried in an avalanche. The receiving beacons interpret the victim's signal into audible and visual displays sent from under the snow to guide searchers. They are deemed by today's winter wilderness travelers to be as necessary as gloves.

Some cross-country ski poles today are designed to be disassembled and combined into avalanche probes to find victims under the snow. There are also now packs that can be triggered to inflate from a gas canister by someone caught in an avalanche. This "avalanche airbag" may be successful in buoying a potential victim to the top of an avalanche to prevent smothering. The majority of avalanche fatalities are caused by asphyxiation.

Second in avalanche deadliness, however, are smashing injuries from being swept into trees or rocks or even over cliffs. Inflating packs might protect from such injuries, but they offer less protection from blunt force trauma than do the automobile airbags that they imitate. Given that this particular cornice collapse not only buried the climbers but also cast them down many feet to rocks, beacons and inflating packs likely would not have helped save their lives.

The pattern of open, gentle slope to the west on Flattop which ended at cliffs on the east face created the ice wall in the shady gully that the victims wanted to climb. The same topography also formed dangerous cornices waiting to flush climbers down the gully without warning. Little the climbers could have done, except not climb, would have helped to eliminate danger from cornice collapse.

Keeping as quiet as possible might have alerted the climbers to a crunching rumble of a cornice crumbling into an avalanche. Clinging to an ice wall would have given them no time to escape the path of falling ice and snow, but it might have given them time to grab for whatever slick surface seemed strongest. A quick prayer would have been the most effective protection from the mass hit. On the other hand, wind howling at the top of the couloir might have drowned the sound of an avalanche, even it if could not prevent a prayer from being heard.

Roaring tons of concrete might have created a greater impact on the climbers, but not by much. Nonetheless, a "hasty search" by the two female watchers might have been appropriate, even, in retrospect, if not very useful. Had their vision not been blocked by a cloud of snow, they could have mentally marked with some point of reference where the climbers were when the avalanche began.

At the same time, they might have noticed where the climbers disappeared on the moving surface of the avalanche and watched that moving point until the avalanche came to rest. Somewhere along a line between those two points the victims would be buried, most likely nearer the bottom point.

The two women then could have divided responsibility with knowledge that a second cornice collapse could be expected to follow the first. One woman might have done sentry duty to shout a warning to the bolder woman as she rushed toward the lower point along the victims' line of fall, watching for lost gear. She could have given special attention to rock outcrops and scanned beneath blocks of snow on the surface of the slide. Both women could have shouted from time to time and then kept absolutely quiet, listening for a muffled reply.

Hopefully, they might have known that snow slides like flowing water, with more speed on the surface of the flow and in the center than along the sides. If the avalanche had followed a twisting path, unlikely when confined by the couloir, the victims would have followed the same turns. Therefore, the women would not have wasted extremely precious time searching within the curves.

Had any of the climbers' equipment appeared on or near the surface of the snow, the most likely place to probe or dig would have been slightly uphill. Lacking any equipment hints, the search should have begun just above the slide's stopping point in the direction of the point where the climbers disappeared. If scratching and digging for the climbers failed to locate a body, probing should have begun at once. (Lack of oxygen and compression of the chest by heavy snow could cause suffocation quickly, even if a victim had managed to preserve breathing space in front of his face during the fall; after the fall, the victim could not move significantly to improve breathing.)

Probing could have been done with long sticks or branches in the unlikely case any were available. Hopefully, ski poles could be reversed to plunge into the snow. Even better would be ice axes with their points blanketed by tape. Sharp probes might pierce a living victim.

If these immediate methods did not work, the women should not have rushed for help, because it would be impossible for it to arrive in time. Rather, it would be necessary to begin a more systematic search, ideally with far more participants than were present. With only two, the sentry would have to join the search, risking another avalanche. The two would stand three feet apart, facing uphill from where the avalanche stopped. At one of the searcher's command, both would plunge their probes into the snow as deeply as possible. The first probe would be a foot in front, the second a foot to the right, the third a foot to the left. Clearly, more searchers would have covered more distance across the slide. By nonvocal signal, the searchers should have proceeded uphill. The searchers would need to move by signal while listening for a victim's voice (unlikely, but possible).

Probing should not have continued beyond the upper point where a victim was seen last. Instead, the whole exhausting procedure should have shifted to the side. Extending the search beyond the fall line might have been appropriate because the victims might have been sidetracked by an eddy.

If probing did not succeed, the only alternative would have been digging trenches with shovels. This likely is a daylong procedure in danger of future avalanches. Experienced backcountry winter travel groups often carry avalanche shovels (one each because a buried shovel is useless). These also are useful after a victim has been located with a probe. The face should be uncovered first and mouth-to-mouth respiration attempted if the victim is not breathing. Simultaneous treatment for freezing, shock, and physical battering is important, but the first priority is breathing. Stubbornness by rescuers might be rewarded even after hours of diminishing hope.

At some point, of course, someone needed to go for help. If hope for a victim had remained or the victim had even been uncovered alive, one woman would have needed to rush to Bear Lake while the other remained to tend to the injured victim. If available, two messengers would have been better both for safety and for obtaining help at Bear Lake.

Because rushing for help is inevitably exhausting after a shocking experience, writing a message for search and rescue teams before leaving the avalanche site may be extremely useful. Under such trying circumstances, forgetfulness is normal. Thus, a notebook and pencil might be as important for avalanche rescue as a shovel and probe. The route from the avalanche site should have been marked in case the site is not well known to rescuers; wind and additional snow could eliminate tracks.

Garbled oral messages could cause rescue failure. Written instructions for search and rescue teams need to include these items:

1. When and where the avalanche occurred.
2. The number of victims and how seriously they were injured.
3. How far from the road and how difficult the terrain is, to indicate the difficulty of recovery.
4. How many people remained at the scene and their conditions.
5. Whether the remaining people at the scene would have to move away from subsequent avalanche danger.
6. Whether the evacuation will require a rigid litter, sliding on a sled, or lowering down cliffs.
7. Because the messengers likely will be in no condition to return immediately with the rescuers, the messengers' location should be made known to the team leader, who might need more information.
8. A list of the names and contact information for victims' families or friends.

At the time this avalanche occurred, using cellphones to call for aid was some years in the future. Even today, cellphone coverage in the Rockies is spotty. Of course, if the only phone is buried, it is unavailable to use even if coverage does reach the avalanche site.

Unpredictable

———

There are two types of avalanches: bad and worse. Wet and dry. Fatal and survived. Technically, slab (most of them) and loose snow. Practically, there is only one type of avalanche: unpredictable.

As a handy generalization, avalanches might occur on any slope gentle enough for snow to accumulate and steep enough to pull a skier downhill. A wide variety of causes can trigger an avalanche. Two additional causes exist in Yellowstone National Park: geothermal activity and earthquake.

This is the story of two extremely experienced cross-country skiers researching geothermal activity in 1997 who died in an avalanche. This, in turn, triggered a massive search for them.

One of these geologists was a park employee who had been researching geysers and hot springs in Yellowstone for twenty-seven years. The other geologist was a volunteer employed in Massachusetts, who had helped develop computer projects involving Yellowstone thermal features. She had taken a month off to help with further research.

On March 1, when the bitter frigidity of Yellowstone winter had begun to diminish, they snowmobiled to the Heart Lake Trailhead. They then snapped on cross-country skis to travel another eight miles to reach the Heart Lake Geyser Basin, where they took shelter from the still considerable cold in the National Park Service's Heart Lake Patrol Cabin. Warmed by a fire they started in the cabin's woodstove, they prepared a meal and plans for their study. On Sunday, March 2, they monitored thermal features in the vicinity of the cabin.

At 8:00 a.m. on Monday, March 3, they radioed park headquarters on Yellowstone's northern edge to conform to the normal policy of confirming that they were safe while traveling through winter wilderness. They arranged to meet two rangers halfway between Heart Lake and the trailhead on March 4. This rendezvous never took place.

Neither did the geologists check in by radio. The rangers skiing all the way to the patrol cabin reported by radio that the snow conditions seemed ominous, whomping and collapsing. *Whomping* indicated the formation of slabs, which are layers of snow that separate from each other and slide downhill. *Collapsing* referred to the slabs in the process of sliding, or cornices of wind-deposited snow unsupported underneath yielding to gravity. When the rangers arrived at the cabin, they deduced that the geologists had not been there since the previous day.

The rangers had passed recent avalanche zones around 2:30 p.m. on the way to the lake at the base of eight-hundred-foot Factory Hill. They had seen ski tracks but pushed on to the cabin to determine if the geologists were there.

When they didn't find them there, the rangers feared the worst and radioed headquarters to report what they had discovered. They then skied back to the avalanche areas to search. More detailed tracking told them that the geologists had skied in and out of the avalanche zone closest to the cabin, which was a relatively small snow slide. Much worse, the researchers' ski tracks entered the much larger avalanche zone at Factory Hill but did not leave it.

Daylight was diminishing, and the weather was getting worse. The rangers knew that two treasured members of the Yellowstone community very likely had perished. They postponed further search efforts until Wednesday morning, when they knew searchers would flock to the area.

Indeed, the next morning a famous rescue ranger arrived from Grand Teton National Park, a short way south of Yellowstone, equipped with explosive charges to immediately jar loose incipient avalanches that threatened searchers in a park that already experienced thousands of earthquake shakings a year. Four canine search and rescue teams arrived to aid more than thirty human searchers thrusting poles into the avalanche site. All was in vain. By the end of the day, helicopters had brought another canine team and more searchers.

Layers of snow in Yellowstone are ready to avalanche.

By Thursday approximately fifty searchers were on-site together with eight search dog teams. Close to evening, they found a ski pole belonging to the park's geologist. Shortly thereafter, a probe hit his body under four feet of snow.

The following morning a helicopter flew out with the NPS geologist's body. It took until 11:40 a.m. to locate the volunteer geologist's body about fifty feet above where the avalanche had swept her fellow researcher. She was under seven feet of snow.

Subsequent investigation surmised that the two researchers had skied across the base (toe) of the waiting avalanche, perhaps cutting whatever delicate mechanics were holding the mass in place. Yet they were on a relatively flat valley floor eight hundred feet below where the avalanche broke loose from a cliffy slope to kill them.

How could their weight crossing a nearly level surface below Factory Hill have triggered such disaster? Perhaps the sunshine of lengthening spring days melted a bit of snow to lubricate the remainder's response to gravity, or an imperceptible tremor in a naturally shaky area broke loose the slabs of snow, or a multitude of causes coincidentally combined.

Perhaps, though experienced, the two skiers were closer together in a seemingly secure zone than the thirty-some yards that might have left one unburied to rescue the other. For an unburied skier, the challenge of digging out a companion swept to an inexact location below seven or four feet of snow, under the threat of another unpredictable avalanche, would have been very difficult. And even with a fast reaction by the victim of preserving breathing space in front of the face, survival for more than a half hour would have been unlikely. Unless a nearby survivor was ready to wield an avalanche shovel, after locating the victim with a probe or avalanche beacon, rescue was likely to convert to recovery. Had two very experienced backcountry skiers remembered that avalanches are unpredictable and remained separated, one might have remained uncovered with a chance of rescuing the other.

IN HOT WATER

Boiling Hot in Bitter Cold

—————

The contrast between very cold air and very hot water paints winter landscapes in Yellowstone National Park with extreme drama. Steam rising from more than ten thousand hot springs fills geyser basins with vapor hovering mysteriously above naked ground, highlighted by snow and the colorful chemistry of thermal activity. It is exciting to experience.

Excitement turned deadly on February 8, 1988. Five employees at Snow Lodge, a winter visitor facility near Old Faithful Geyser, were camping on the shore of Shoshone Lake about eleven miles south of the famous symbol of Yellowstone. All had the winter camping experience and good physical conditioning anticipated among concessionaire employees who provided care for park visitors arriving by tracked snow coaches or snowmobiles a day's travel from any plowed road.

The campers used their cross-country skiing skills to reach the even more remote Shoshone Geyser Basin, cleared of deep snow by the boiling hot springs. The National Park Service had assigned them a legal campsite away from the shore of Shoshone Lake. Influenced by the threat of an incoming storm, the skiers chose to camp instead on the lake's beach, where their location was unknown. (NPS-designated backcountry campsites normally are not adjacent to lakes or streams in order to prevent damage to these heavily trafficked areas.)

For some reason (nature appreciation, contemplation, illegal soaking in some rare hot spring not hot enough to kill), John Mark Williams left his four friends around 5:00 p.m. as they set up camp in gathering dusk. When

Opposite: Castle Geyser exemplifies the drama of boiling water expelled into frigid winter air.

the others turned down his suggestion of company, Williams walked into the Shoshone Geyser Basin alone in a light snowfall. By 6:00 the snow was increasing; the four cleaned their dinner pots and retreated to the warmth of sleeping bags in their tent. They emerged in full dark to look for Williams as gales filled with blowing snow. Their lights could not penetrate the blizzard, and they gave up searching after ten confusing minutes, still concerned about Williams but also confident about his ability to care for himself.

Around 7:30 p.m., distant screams penetrated the tent. Squirming out of their sleeping bags and then outside, the campers heard more screams for help and saw Williams stumbling swiftly toward them with his hands in the air. He was crying that he had fallen into a very hot spring and was in great pain.

His friends removed his wet clothes and placed him in a sleeping bag. From his feet to his neck, he was covered in second and third degree burns. Long strips of skin already were peeling from 90 percent of his body. The other four elevated his feet to moderate the effects of shock as his screams pierced the tent and shattered the night in conjunction with howling wind.

Two campers set out for help, skiing together in an approximation of safety. They hoped to reach two Park Service rangers they knew were staying at a patrol cabin near the lake three miles away. But its exact location was unknown to them, and the bulb on one of two headlamps burned out. Well-equipped, they had a replacement bulb; it broke, leaving them with only one light growing ever dimmer in absolute blizzard blackness.

To conserve what remained of the battery, they turned the headlamp off and strove to ski blind. They came upon the fast-disappearing ski tracks of the two rangers, but soon lost them amid fresh snow and frequent falls. They yelled constantly for the rangers, who had no reason to leave the shelter of their cabin and could not hear them. Close-growing lodgepole pines extended low branches to jab and snare in the howling gale. A mile away, Williams's cries of agony from the tent lashed them like the wind.

Finally, the two messengers of disaster decided to give up trying to find the patrol cabin and instead follow the rapidly disappearing tracks of their ski group back eleven miles to Snow Lodge. After three miles, energy failed for one of the skiers around 10:45 p.m., and she collapsed. She called to the other for help. He assisted her to find some shelter beneath a large tree, where she spent a deeply uncomfortable night of fear while her companion pushed on unencumbered by her slowness. The next day she skied alone back to Old Faithful in psychological misery.

As her stronger companion skied through the night, he kept the blowing snow at his back to maintain the right direction. Snow and wind hid the route through the woods, so he made his way to the bank of the Firehole River, still flowing in twenty-degree temperature due to water coming in from the two-hundred-degree hot springs. Following the sound of flowing water, he arrived at Old Faithful by 4:00 a.m. A security guard called the park's chief ranger, and the Park Service began search and rescue operations. These were delayed until daylight to avoid added danger to rescuers.

More than twenty rangers and volunteers began at 7:30 a.m. to fight their way through the blizzard from the park's south and west entrances. By far the closest were two rangers, one also a medic, whom Williams's companions had been unable to find at Shoshone Lake. Word of the accident finally got to these rangers by radio at 8:00, and they began skiing with rescue supplies, including oxygen, across Shoshone Lake, covered by masses of untracked snow.

The two rangers tried to keep in contact by radio with other rangers but gave up because reception was bad and trying to get more information slowed their progress. At 10:30 a.m. they reached Shoshone Geyser Basin and radioed for the location of the campsite, not knowing that the campers' tent was not at the legal site.

They found the hot pool where Williams had fallen in, identified by a floating water bottle and scattered clothing. For the next fifty minutes, the rescuers floundered around, sometimes separating, looking in vain for the tent when all tracks had been wiped out by the blizzard. Finally, a guess led them to look on the beach instead of in the woods where the campers were supposed to be. About a half hour later, they radioed the park headquarters that they had found the tent. It was too late.

When they approached the tent, yelling, the two survivors crawled from the tent, crying.

As has been typical with hot spring deaths in Yellowstone, the victim's end had been long in coming and of indescribable agony. The two women remaining with Williams had served him well. They fought deadly dehydration with all the juice they had, then water, then snow melted in their mouths when wind prevented use of their backpacking stove. They tried to keep him warm when fierce wind blew the tent's zipper apart. They kept containers of snow next to their skin in hopes of melting more water for him. They held him as he screamed and thanked them for their help. They tried artificial respiration as his lungs filled with fluid. They prayed. They kissed his forehead and closed his eyes when peace came at last with death, likely around 9:50 a.m.

When the two rangers finally found the tent shortly before noon, they immediately attempted artificial respiration. They described his appearance in great detail to a physician over their radio. At 12:25 p.m., the doctor determined that Williams was dead.

Other rescuers soon arrived, all having missed finding Williams alive by approximately two hours. The hot spring into which he had fallen was nameless, very near Black Sulphur Spring. The deadly pool was measured at 187 degrees Fahrenheit and eight feet deep. All the elements of the incident taken into account, nothing the rangers or Williams's companions could have done would have saved him. He was doomed as soon as he fell into the hot spring.

Futile

———

Rangers in Yellowstone are very serious about protecting visitors from danger (as well as protecting the park from visitors) in unusual and unfamiliar terrain. In 2016, rangers had prevented for sixteen years anyone from being scalded to death in the hot springs that the park had been created to protect. They have a tough job enforcing wisdom in the face of ignorance.

Predictably, among the millions of visitors seeking to experience one of the world's greatest natural wonders, there was one twenty-three-year-old who refused to be hogtied by regulations. He and his sister left a safe boardwalk above the hot springs in Norris Geyser Basin, and walked more than the length of two football fields over what looked like solid ground. As obvious National Park Service signs tried to inform them, it was not the normal solid ground of their previous experience. It was only a thin crust above acid water that at times had been measured at 459 degrees Fahrenheit, hotter than any of Yellowstone's other hot springs that have been measured at merely the boiling point.

At a four-foot-wide hot spring near Porkchop Geyser, the brother approached the pool's edge to determine if it was cool enough to enter for illegal soaking, locally called "hot potting." Perhaps the thin crust broke beneath his weight. Or maybe he slipped.

As soon as he tumbled into the boiling water, his sister, of course, ran for help and managed to return safely to the boardwalk. A park search and rescue team risked their lives venturing over dangerous volcanic terrain to the accident site but could retrieve only the brother's flip-flops floating in the water. (Even heavy leather hiking boots will not protect feet from the

Norris Geyser Basin is an especially hot geothermal area in Yellowstone.

boiling water of Yellowstone hot springs. As further demonstration of the frustrating task rangers face in protecting all park visitors, flip-flops provide negligible foot protection for walking across a Yellowstone parking lot to a boardwalk or for walking across Old Faithful Inn's elegant lobby.)

A fierce lightning storm threatening death from above drove the ranger search and rescue team from further attempts to retrieve the brother. They knew their efforts in the face of the extreme nature of the accident were futile. The brother's body dissolved in the acid water; there was nothing to recover.

HYPOTHERMIA

Vaille Fail

I'll do it if it kills me" is an exaggerated cliché that most people have heard or even said. Although Agnes Wollcott Vaille may never have said these words about her desire to be the first person to climb the 1,800-foot-high East Face of Longs Peak in a Colorado winter, the passion the saying expresses burned within her in January 1925. She did climb the East Face in winter. It did kill her. It also killed Herbert Sortland, who failed to rescue her.

A modern depiction of climbing routes up the East Face has stripes draped so thickly that the picture appears to show almost more white lines than buff granite. Such was not the case in 1925, when few climbers even in summer had pioneered the least difficult ascents of the sheer cliff on Colorado's most conspicuous fourteen-thousand-foot peak. None had succeeded in winter.

Not even thirty-four-year-old Agnes Vaille, graduate of Smith College, secretary of the Denver Chamber of Commerce, and enthusiastic naturalist with the Colorado Mountain Club (CMC), had been able to scale the East Face in winter. She had failed in partnership with Walter Kiener, a recent Swiss immigrant whom she met in the CMC. In each of the last three months of 1924, Longs Peak, the highest in Rocky Mountain National Park, turned them back. They made it to the top on the fatal fourth try, climbing up what is still called Kiener's Route, the least difficult way to ascend the East Face.

The last climb began on January 11 with a too late start, delayed by snow on the road from Denver. They began a night hike to Timberline Cabin, a drafty shelter at tree line (no longer standing). Hiking with them was Elinor Eppich, who four decades later would coauthor with Louisa Arps the grandly researched book *High Country Names* about the origins of names of landmarks in Rocky Mountain National Park and adjacent Indian Peaks Wilderness.

With scant sleep, Kiener and Vaille waited for a storm to seemingly clear before beginning at 9:00 a.m. (again too late) the hike to the base of the East Face above Chasm Lake. Eppich began hiking down to Longs Peak Inn to wait for the climbers' return. When they had not returned by the next morning, Eppich sounded the alarm, recruiting four rescuers from among employees at the inn.

Soon after they arrived at Timberline Cabin, Kiener staggered in from a vicious winter storm that had arrived with one-hundred-mile-per-hour wind. He carried a tale of disaster.

Vaille and Kiener, after their late start, had climbed all day on January 11 and continued through the night. The gale began and dropped the effective temperature to fourteen degrees below zero. Climbing a vertical slab for hundreds of feet in the dark of winter must have added energy-sapping fear to their physical exertion. However, they did summit around 4:00 a.m. on January 12, which wasn't bad time, everything considered.

Winter winds rake Longs Peak with snow.

Their hands were too frozen to sign a summit register, but this likely was not a high priority at that point.

The two climbers chose the shortest escape route (although not the easiest) down Longs's North Face. Unsurprisingly after an extremely tiring climb, Vaille slipped. She landed on snow and slid 150 feet, stopping uninjured but totally exhausted. Kiener was able to help her to the completely level Boulderfield at the base of the North Face, but she could go no farther.

The Swiss climber had no strength remaining to carry her across a very unstable and difficult surface of huge rocks, so he left her in as sheltered a place as possible and hurried away for aid. His feet were frozen. Nonetheless, he led the searchers as they headed out from the drafty cabin into the immensely worse gale conditions to rescue Vaille.

So rapid had been the searchers' response to Eppich's call for help, they had left Longs Peak Inn ill-equipped to face winter gales. One searcher could continue for only a short way. He instructed another searcher who had remained at the cabin to keep a fire burning, then descended to the inn to look for more help. A third searcher, twenty-two-year-old Herbert Sortland (a caretaker at Longs Peak Inn) also was forced to retreat before reaching the immense Boulderfield.

Kiener, close to walking death, strove on heroically with one remaining searcher. They found Agnes Vaille about a hundred feet from where Kiener had left her. She had fallen on the tippy boulders and landed face down, arms outstretched (easy enough to do even while unexhausted in warm summer daylight). Likely she had died within an hour after the fall from cold and exhaustion.

Kiener, by now snowblind (evidently unequipped with goggles), frostbitten, and far beyond worn out, was an excellent candidate to be the next fatality. The remaining searcher led him back to the cabin's semi-warmth and rescued him from death.

At the end of the short winter day, three National Park Service rangers arrived at the cabin. Kiener told them that Vaille was dead back in the Boulderfield. Obviously, the searcher who had carried news of the disaster had made it back to the inn because the rangers had hiked to the cabin.

But no one had seen Herbert Sortland after he was forced back down the mountain.

At 4:00 a.m. park superintendent Roger Toll (Vaille's cousin) and his successor, Edmund Rogers, arrived. Four miles had been added to their trek because the storm had closed the road to Longs Peak Inn. Icicles hung from their noses and chins. A ranger slit the frostbite blisters on Kiener's hands in an effort to reduce the pain.

At last, they all hiked down to the inn. An ambulance managed to take Kiener down to a hospital in Denver, where he remained for four months. Parts of all his fingers, save one, most of his toes, and part of one foot were amputated. Vaille's family, in gratitude, paid most of Kiener's medical expenses.

Superintendent Toll, grateful for Kiener's heroic suffering in attempting to save Vaille, hired the Swiss as a ranger. His duty provided healing time as he sat in a fire lookout atop Twin Sisters Peak with a spectacular view of Longs Peak's East Face across the Tahosa Valley. Later, Kiener enrolled at the University of Nebraska to study biology, again with financial help from Vaille's family. He specialized in alpine vegetation.

An immediate, intensive search for Herbert Sortland failed to locate him. As often is the case when a lone traveler in the wilds disappears, his body was found accidentally, six weeks after Vaille's death. While hauling garbage to a Longs Peak Inn dump, an inn employee discovered the searcher melting out of a snowbank. He had fallen somewhere on the descent and dislocated his hip. In great pain, he had failed by about three hundred yards to reach the inn and had frozen to death.

After the storm that had killed Vaille abated, Superintendent Toll with family and friends retrieved her body on January 15 with a litter improvised from skis. Toll was disturbed by Vaille's death not only because his cousin had died in a venture of questionable merit, but also because he assumed it was his responsibility to protect park visitors.

Kiener suggested that cables installed at difficult spots on the North Face would make it easier to ascend or descend. Toll agreed and had a route cleared of loose stones. Holes drilled in the rock received large rods with eyes on the ends to hold the cable handrails. Decades later, the wire ropes had frayed so much that the Park Service would have to replace them or eliminate them. Over a half century, park administrators began to see the cables as an unnatural intrusion in the wilderness and removed them in 1993.

Toll also saw a need for a shelter cabin in the Boulderfield. It was two stories, constructed of the plentiful stone on hand, and could shelter dozens of climbers in a pinch. Turned over to a concessionaire, it was dubbed the highest hotel in the world (12,700 feet above sea level). But the freeze and thaw of water trickling amid the huge rocks on which it was built destroyed the structure in the 1930s. Its ruins have disappeared.

In 1926 and 1927, Vaille's family constructed another stone shelter at the Keyhole, a notch of that shape in the ridge extending between the peak's North and West Faces to Stones Peak. It is a relatively small gap that nonetheless is easy to see from miles away. This shelter hut looks something like the corn-storage structures motorists from the East might see in agriculture fields on the way to Colorado. It has a plain concrete floor and the inside is blackened, surely from the smoke of backpacking stoves, for wood fuel is miles distant.

In sight of where Agnes Vaille died, the hut bears a bronze plate commemorating her memory and that of her attempted rescuer, Herbert Sortland. The plaque reads:

Agnes Wolcott Vaille

This shelter commemorates a Colorado mountaineer
conquered by winter after scaling the precipice January 12,
1925, and one who lost his life in an effort to save her.

Herbert Sortland

Built on the shady North Face, the shelter is colder than the sunny West Face a few feet away, but it has comforted thousands and perhaps rescued some climbers. It may be the highest-altitude structure within the US National Park System.

Cellphones on the Grand

Climbing routes cover the Grand Teton like icing on a Bundt cake. But some routes are not so sweet at particular times and seasons.

The Grand Teton, one of the world's most famous mountains, has cellphone coverage because it is the highest point in its vicinity. Therefore, climbers attempting to scale the Grand in one day instead of the normal two were able to call the National Park Service in Wyoming's Grand Teton National Park at 8:15 p.m. one Saturday in 2015 to report they were in trouble. The sun was setting; they had not made the summit; their ropes were stuck, preventing further descent; and they were soaked in melting snow with deadly hypothermia imminent for some climbers.

Why had they attempted a one-day ascent? Perhaps they sought to jam as many great experiences into life as possible and therefore climb another mountain on the following day or float in a raft down the Snake River. The next day being Sunday, perhaps they wished to worship in the delightful and famous Chapel of the Transfiguration, which commemorates the ascent of a high mountain by Jesus and a few friends, where he was transfigured before them. Perhaps they could take only one day off from selling souvenirs to tourists during busy August, or perhaps they had to mow lawns.

The two stranded parties were large (four and six) for climbing the Grand. Climbing with so many friends was more fun but less speedy, and many other people wanted to climb the Grand on an August weekend, some having traveled long distances to do so. Any route up the Grand is often narrow in spots and requires waiting for other climbers to pass, like a post office the week before Christmas. Even utilizing the outhouse on the Lower Saddle might take half an hour.

Reaching the Lower Saddle via Garnet Canyon in time to head for the summit by 7:00 a.m. was a good start for the two parties. But the summit was a long, laborious, slow 2,083 feet higher. At least by hiking in predawn darkness they avoided the energy-draining heat that often is encountered on the shadeless trail leading to the Lower Saddle. This benefit was not adequate to overcome their subsequent delays, however, and at nightfall NPS received a call for help.

It was much too late in the day to extract ten climbers by short-haul helicopter. This extraction technique can remove injured or stuck climbers from the mountain in hours rather than days, saving lives. NPS describes the short-haul as "a rescue procedure where an individual or gear is suspended below the helicopter by a 150- to 200-foot rope. This method allows a rescuer more direct access to an injured party, and it is used in the Teton Range where conditions make it difficult to land a heli-copter in the steep and rocky terrain." ("Difficult to land a helicopter" is an understatement likely to incite smirks among those who are familiar with the terrain.)

The two climbing parties united on part of the route called Petzoldt Ridge and decided to retreat by rappelling (or sliding down a rope) in Chevy Couloir and into Stettner Couloir to descend to the Lower Sad-dle. They had not sufficiently researched their escape route to realize that Stettner Couloir in summer's heat became a waterfall of melting snow with wet, steep, water-polished walls. (*Couloir* is a climbing term for a vertical-trending gully.) These conditions soon made the climbers soaked and cold, putting them at risk for hypothermia, which is when the body temperature goes below ninety-six degrees. Hypothermia can reduce mental ability and lead to death of even experienced climbers. (Modern analysis of the effects has substituted the term *hypothermia* for what formerly was called *freezing* or *exposure*.) Moreover, the snowmelt loosened sizable rocks to send them crashing down to potentially strike the stranded climbers.

Unable to send in a helicopter, the National Park Service sent one of their Jenny Lake Climbing Rangers up the trail to the Lower Saddle. He made the hike of seven miles in the dark over frequently rough and very steep terrain with an elevation gain of nearly five thousand feet. There would be little he could do on reaching the Lower Saddle except administer first aid.

More helpful search and rescue operations would have to wait for dawn's early light on Sunday. Rangers on the phone urged the climbers to either descend Stettner Couloir or get out of its water in some safer, drier place to share body warmth. At 11:30 p.m. the climbers called to inform the rangers that the two climbing groups were uniting to try to descend the couloirs to reach the Lower Saddle by morning. Two of the combined group did make it down about an hour later with news about the trials of their companions.

Some of the climbers, in attempting to rescue themselves, became so tired or wet that their partners feared them to be hypothermic. Therefore, most of the group decided to halt their climb down until they could see. Early light at 5:50 a.m. brought another call to the rangers that the stranded climbers were stuck in the couloirs and needed to get warm and dry as soon as possible.

At this time, two rangers then in the Lower Saddle began climbing toward the stranded group. Once with the climbers, the rangers hoped to figure out if helicopter evacuation was possible. However, strong winds kept the helicopter on the ground. Three more rangers, therefore, hiked to the Lower Saddle to support a ground rescue. When the high winds diminished, a helicopter carried an additional three rangers to the Lower Saddle to take part in the rescue.

Rangers also encountered four professional climbing guides and two other climbers nearby who could help. One ranger and two volunteers ascended to the rescue site. The professional guides set up an aid point to cross a section of the climbing route below Stettner Couloir ominously called the Black Dike, named for a crack in the Grand's gray granite that filled with a flow of black diabase (a very hard, dark-colored igneous rock) during the mountain's formation.

When everyone was finally back down to the Lower Saddle in the early afternoon, rangers served them food and hot drink (the fastest way to offset

The Teton Range attracts many climbers and batters some of them.

hypothermia) and checked them for further need for care. They decided that four of the climbers needed immediate evacuation by helicopter to the valley floor, and the remaining six were fit to hike out on their own. NPS rangers with a helicopter and competent volunteer help had rescued ten climbers uninjured from the perils of hypothermia and gravity.

Seventeen Years

———

D r. Thornton Rogers Sampson was a clergyman, a scholar, and an edu-
cator—a surprisingly typical mountaineer in the Colorado Rockies
during the early twentieth century. If asked the title of his favorite guide-
book, he likely would have responded with "The Bible" and quoted Psalms
121: "I lift my eyes unto the hills . . ."

Perhaps Dr. Sampson intended to hike over the Continental Divide
from the west side of the mountains on September 2, 1915, in order to
attend dedication ceremonies for the newly established Rocky Mountain
National Park. He did hike over Flattop Mountain, but then he disappeared
for seventeen years.

Sampson was born in 1852 and survived to adulthood through the Civil
War, not a common feat when bullets were flying thickly in Virginia. At
age nineteen, he entered university in Virginia to study Greek (the original
New Testament language) and moral philosophy, at the time necessities for
a future minister. He sailed to Europe in 1874 for education in Edinburgh,
Scotland, and Leipzig, Germany, then leading centers of theology, and
moved on to further study in the Middle East, where Christianity began.

He returned to the United States in 1878, was married, and then
ordained into the Presbyterian ministry. He and his wife soon set off for
missionary work in Greece, India, Ceylon, Japan, Korea, and China. He was
an enthusiast, obviously.

In 1894 Dr. Sampson took on the presidency of Fredericksburg College, near Austin, Texas, and in three years had placed the college on a
much more substantial economic foundation. He then moved to Sherman,
Texas, to become president of Austin College. In 1900 he helped found a

Presbyterian seminary in Austin, resigning from its presidency to become its Luther Professor of Church History and Polity. In 1912, like so many Texas residents then as now, Sampson discovered the Colorado Rockies and became even more of an enthusiast.

On August 7, 1915, the Sampsons arrived in Denver and traveled to the YMCA of the Rockies to lodge on the eastern edge of the new Rocky Mountain National Park. Sampson set off alone on August 11 for a three-week fishing and camping journey through the region around Estes Park Village adjacent to the national park. His wife returned to Denver.

He must have done very little fishing and a great deal of traveling, for a week later he sent his wife a postcard from Rand, Colorado, a long way north and west of Estes Park. He sent another postcard from Rand on August 21, indicating that he was headed to visit friends near Cameron Pass, west of the town of Fort Collins. Another postcard mailed from Cameron Pass on the 28th indicated that he never had felt better in his life and was gaining in strength and health. He seemed destined for superherohood, but it was his final communication with anyone.

Subsequent investigation indicated that Sampson had continued a fervent pace down to Squeaky Bob Wheeler's tent resort camp some halfway south in the national park and then on to the town of Grand Lake by September 1. On September 2 a horseback rider encountered Sampson on the North Inlet Trail to Estes Park, where he may have intended to attend national park founding festivities on September 4. The rider gave Sampson directions to Fern Lake Lodge in the national park on the east side of the Continental Divide via Flattop Mountain.

By 2:00 p.m. westbound hikers saw Sampson resting on the east side of Flattop about six miles from Fern Lake Lodge. By 4:00 fair weather had become heavy snow blown by high wind, with dense clouds dropping to engulf Flattop in fog. Nonetheless, Sampson's horseback informant gave him good directions, even anchoring a scarf atop a pile of rocks to indicate where the hiker should cut left from the trail to follow a vague route through Odessa Gorge down to the lodge.

No one in the large park dedication crowd on September 4 expected Sampson or missed him when he was not there. When he failed to show up in Denver as scheduled on September 5, his wife and friends were not concerned. His enthusiasm did not lend itself to a strict timetable.

But when he still was absent on September 13, a determined search and rescue effort began. Hikers very familiar with the area scouted Odessa Gorge and the Continental Divide as far west as Specimen Mountain (an extremely distant part of the Divide for disaster to have overtaken Sampson, but any conceivable site was explored). Weather increased the searchers' problem. One group camped in a foot of snow at Bear Lake on a different flank of Flattop from Odessa Gorge.

By September 18 more than fifteen searchers were seeking Sampson. His wife offered a $500 reward (1915 dollars) for his discovery alive or dead. Also on the 18th, the US Forest Service deployed twenty rangers into the search. They searched without success for five days along the Continental Divide.

Sampson's son, who doubtless had heard many of his father's sermons, wrote in the *Rocky Mountain News* on September 19 (before the Forest Service searchers had given up), "Father loved the mountains. He said he communed with the highest things while alone in the depths of wild, rugged country. And, if father's time had been allotted, what more could he have asked than to have stood alone with his Maker on top of the peak and give his tired spirit to Him whose hand alone guided him in the night of snow, cold, and peril?"

All of this doubtless was true as well as comforting to the Sampson family. But the most relevant words in this comment were the two uses of "alone."

Seventeen years later, on July 8, 1932, a national park trail crew surveying a trail to be built through Odessa Gorge found Dr. Sampson's skeleton. It was identified by the contents in a small pack under an overhanging rock on a slope above Fern Lake Lodge. Sampson had followed expertly the good directions given him and started down Odessa Gorge. While traversing a broad band of loose rock crossing his route, attacked by snow and growing darkness, he fell and broke his shin bone.

It was an incapacitating injury, generating pain similar to that caused to his Master by crucifixion. Nonetheless, Sampson managed to make his way

Dr. Sampson suffered a broken shin while descending Odessa Gorge.

to a sort of sheltered place and even make a fire. The blaze could not protect him from his pain, wet clothes, and the cold of high altitude at night. He fell asleep and froze to death as his body temperature dropped below the point needed for life.

After the discovery, his son wrote, "I cannot imagine father wishing for a more peaceful passing—high in the mountains from which all his life he drew his inspiration."

The inspiration was certain, but his passing was not peaceful. He fought it through severe pain by crawling to some shelter and starting a fire, the fuel for which must have been difficult to assemble. His son maintained that the only mistake his father made was going to sleep, as though his father had any choice.

Instead, his mistake was hiking alone, when any companion could have made it down to Fern Lake to summon lifesaving rescue in order that he could continue his many benefits to society. Perhaps, however, no companion could have had the enthusiasm to keep up with Dr. Sampson.

Too Competent

G ood snow is how skiers, either alpine or cross-country, judge the west side of the Continental Divide. Their evaluation is due to the earth's counterclockwise rotation, which causes prevailing winds from the west at the Rockies' latitude. These winds carry water-laden air from the Pacific Ocean to be eventually emptied when the high mountains push this air to higher, colder elevation where it can hold less water. Therefore, it dumps most of its remaining moisture on the west side of the mountains, creating good snow of sufficient quantity for good skiing.

On March 9, 1980, a group of eight experienced cross-country skiers set out from Grand Lake to take advantage of good snow in climbing 13,310-foot Mount Alice in Colorado's Rocky Mountain National Park. This route from the west was roughly a mile farther than from the east and had a hundred-foot greater elevation gain. But these slight handicaps were offset by good snow and the presence of four lakes along the route. These were, of course, barren of rocks or fallen trees and were absolutely flat, making for easier skiing. Beyond the prosaically named Fourth Lake, however, the route to Boulder-Grand Pass below Mount Alice climbed very steeply.

The route selected to be less radically steep than the others was nonetheless subject to avalanches, thereby prompting each of the eight skiers to carry avalanche shovels designed specifically to rescue any team member unfortunate enough to be buried. For the same reason, all members carried avalanche beacons set on transmit to always send a signal to other beacons that could be set to receive should a search need to begin instantly for anyone buried out of sight. Avalanche shovels also were handy for digging snow caves, much warmer and more secure than uninsulated tents.

The distinct shape of Mount Alice attracts climbers in Rocky Mountain National Park.

The eight skied for five and a half miles up East Inlet Creek to camp in snow caves at Lone Pine Lake. The next morning, they began kicking and gliding together on long, skinny skis for one and four-tenths miles to Lake Verna. Another mile brought them to Spirit Lake and then soon to blandly named Fourth Lake. The skiers continued to push with determination.

Beyond Fourth Lake, they departed from the pleasant East Inlet for the heroic ascent to Boulder-Grand Pass. Very steep even for these experienced ski mountaineers, their climb finally reached the broad pass on the boundary between Boulder and Grand Counties. There they encountered the east slope, where snow was scoured away by near-constant fierce wind. Stashing their skis in a somewhat sheltered spot from which the wind was unlikely to blow them away, the climbers looked up to their goal. Their gasping breath was not due entirely to scant oxygen at the 12,061-foot pass. The bulky tower of Mount Alice still rose 1,249 laborious feet above them. It was a simple trudge from the pass to the peak alongside the top of dramatic cliffs carved long ago by glaciers on the east side of Alice.

The wind was a fairly typical seventy miles per hour, reducing visibility with snow to nearly nothing. Two of the eight decided that a long ski run back down to East Inlet was more appealing and left the group. The remaining six conferred about whether to fight the weather and decided to continue ascending. The remainder of the climb was uncomplicated walking with no cliffs to scale approaching the summit from the west.

Recognizing the danger from the wind, they assured one another of the importance of keeping together. Each of them knew the symptoms of hypothermia, where the body's interior temperature drops below ninety-six degrees due to some assault of cold; for instance, wind sweeping away body heat despite warm clothing. They knew that hypothermia can cause reduced thinking capacity before it kills. But their increased knowledge about their risk likely offset their decreased mental capacity to recognize it.

About a fifteen-minute hike up from the pass, the six stopped for rest and mutual observation. When they started up again, Ruth Magnusson was second from the end of their line. When they stopped again a short way below the summit, she was missing.

Three of the climbers continued to the top, while the two others waited, stating that Magnusson had been with them eight minutes previously. They decided to wait for her to catch up, while the other three proceeded to the summit. When these three returned, Magnusson was still missing.

The group descended to their skis. Her skis still were there, but Magnusson was missing. They knew she was well-equipped, but three skied down to Grand Lake to call for help. The others trudged back up to Boulder-Grand Pass to continue to search for the missing climber, but they were driven back by the wind and blowing snow.

At this point declining mental capacity due to energy depletion and cold may have caused Magnusson's team to fail to recognize her critical danger. She was so experienced and so well-equipped that it was difficult to conceptualize that she was close to dying.

Two National Park Service rangers led a search team toward Boulder-Grand Pass from the nearer east side the next afternoon. They made it as far as a ranger patrol cabin at Thunder Lake against wind that created a forty-degree-below-zero wind chill.

The next morning the rangers climbed by a faint trail four hundred feet in elevation above the lake at the pass to continue their search for

Magnusson. When the wind at last diminished, helicopters brought in fourteen more searchers, including another ranger.

All searchers carried avalanche beacons in the receive mode, hoping to pick up transmission from Magnusson's beacon. Around 2:15 p.m. one of her original climbing team members among the searchers heard her beacon. Her body lay just four hundred yards from the summit. She had died seven hours after disappearing from the group.

Had she become confused by loss of energy from the climb and loss of heat from the wind and become separated from the group? Or had she become separated from the group and then been killed by hypothermia sucking heat from her core? Because all her team members knew she was well-equipped and a competent winter mountaineer, it did not occur to them that she could be in trouble until it was too late.

When mountain travail and elements batter the best climbers, the mind is the first thing to go. The body can carry on into peril after direction from the brain fades away.

LIGHTNING

Longs Peak Lightning

A normal summer starting time for an ascent of Longs Peak, the tallest in Colorado's Rocky Mountain National Park, is 3:30 a.m. So traditional is this start time that, though there likely is parking space available at the trailhead, climbers may form lines at trailhead restrooms.

Of course, this very early start tradition is horrid but, nonetheless, not horrid enough. Far better is a 2:30 or even 2:00 a.m. time to hit the Longs Peak Trail. This very early start likely will put well-conditioned hikers above tree line when alpenglow spreads its spectacle across the mountain's East or North Face for impressive photos. (An interesting silhouette—for instance, a fellow climber or wind-distorted tree—adds interest to the photo.)

A bit more important advantage to a very early start is the chance that National Park Service search and rescue rangers will be less likely to have to remove a body from the peak due to slipping on rain-slickened granite or being struck by lightning. This start time is good for the normal Keyhole route used by most climbers. Climbers choosing the much more difficult routes up the East Face are well-advised to start the previous day and sleep nearer the summit at a designated campsite with an NPS permit.

Two well-conditioned, competent climbers started up the Longs Peak Trail on July 12, 2000, at 3:30 a.m. They were headed for a route difficult even by East Face standards. Perhaps they did not pause to rest or to listen to two possible streamside natural symphonies of running water in the dark. Perhaps they did not bother with composing photos at sunrise, or they cared only for the poetry of rock climbing. Only one hiked back down the trail.

Even with single-minded attention to their goal, it was too tough to complete before a typical afternoon storm gathered around the peak. By 2:30 p.m. they already were so far up the East Face that when wind and clouds marshaled an attack, the climbers felt it was more prudent and faster to push on to the top and head down by a quicker route than to retreat to Chasm Lake hundreds of feet below.

About 3:00 p.m. the lead climber was belaying his partner (protecting him from falling with a rope) in a push toward the top when there was a bright flash but, oddly, no perceptible crash of thunder. (A meteorologist maintains that lightning without thunder is impossible; perhaps the strike briefly deafened the climbers.) The lead climber felt his partner fall and immediately stopped the plunge, belaying on the rope. This arrest was normal.

The lower partner called to the upper that the fall had been caused by his being hit by lightning, he thought. The fallen partner seemed somewhat incoherent. The upper climber let out the belaying rope to lower his partner to a ledge on the often-climbed East Face, where each rare protuberance has been named, in this case the Yellow Wall Bivouac Ledge. The upper climber yelled to the lower to clip into an anchor, a rock-climbing technical term that the lower climber surely understood. But he did not secure himself to the rock wall.

While preparing to rappel (using gear to slide down the rope) to aid his friend, the upper climber felt him fall again and again stopped the fall. He tied the rope holding his partner to an anchor inserted in a crack in the granite and rapelled down to assist him. This action took about ten minutes.

When the upper climber reached the lower, his partner was hanging in his climbing harness. His face was up; his arms and legs were spread out. His complexion was blue; he had no pulse, he was not breathing. The first climber struck his partner twice in the chest in an attempt to restart the heart. The attempt failed. Hanging where eagles soar offered no opportunity for cardiopulmonary resuscitation.

During all this turmoil, the lead climber had been screaming for help. Mountain echo carried his cry to other climbers relatively far away, below

Lightning killed one of two climbers above Chasm Lake on the East Face of Longs Peak.

the North Face in a field of rocks called the Boulderfield. They made their way up a simple but stiff climb to a point called Chasm View, from where they could see the site of the trouble, presumably caused by a lightning strike. They used a cellphone to call the Park Service for help, then shouted to the East Face climber that a helicopter was on the way. Just what good the aircraft could have done under the circumstances was unclear, and the climber shouted back that it was too late. Lightning in a mid-afternoon strike had claimed another climber.

The lead climber rapelled down the cliff face, leaving his dead companion hanging, picked up his cached gear, and hiked back down toward the trailhead. On the way, he met a ranger and told him of the fatality. They then descended together to an NPS office to do death paperwork.

About 5:50 p.m. two rangers boarded a helicopter rented by NPS and checked the climbers' route. They saw the lightning-struck climber hanging from his rope, then flew over the ridge between Longs and Mount Lady Washington to the Boulderfield to interview at 6:07 p.m. the witnesses who first had reported the accident. An hour later the two rangers climbed to a point from which they could observe the victim through binoculars. After fifteen minutes, it seemed obvious that all the witnesses were correct. He was dead.

They recommended by radio to a supervisor that climbing rangers should descend from the summit and another team should raise the body to the broad top of Longs, from which a helicopter could remove it. The next morning at 6:00, a recovery team assembled and learned their assignments. The helicopter ferried three rangers to the summit at 8:00 a.m. to begin setting up rope systems. Eventually, nine team members were flown to the top. The original two rangers would be lowered down the East Face to the body.

Through the morning, fixed ropes and anchors were set in place. Again, as the recovery progressed, the weather got worse. Rain and hail predicted more lightning as water, both liquid and frozen particles, rubbed together to generate more electricity. The helicopter removed the rangers from the summit, where they would be the highest points in the vicinity and, therefore, the most likely lightning targets.

The following morning, a helicopter returned the rescue team to the summit to make use of the preparations set in place the previous day. One of the original rangers rappelled two hundred feet from an overlook above the hanging body to attach haul lines to the lightning victim, while the other original ranger belayed his partner. Arriving alongside the victim, the ranger noticed a burn mark from the lightning strike in the victim's chest.

When the body was hauled up, the climbing ranger, still belayed by his partner, used jumars (technical climbing devices rather like spring-operated pliers attached to slings that allow a climber to ascend a rope like a ladder) to return to the top. From the point from which the ranger had descended, the body was placed in a litter and lifted away by helicopter by 4:00 p.m., with lightning thankfully absent. By 6:10 p.m. all team members and their recovery equipment were removed, restoring the summit to its pristine state.

The whole incident seemed odd. Lightning normally would have been expected to strike the leader, who was higher, rather than the second climber. The victim's being able to discuss his being struck before he suddenly died also seemed strange.

In any case, the feat of the lead climber in rappelling so far down the cliff to escape without aid was impressive. Equally impressive was the smooth and safe carrying out of the recovery operation.

Hurlyburly

―――――

Three groups of climbers began their ascent of Grand Teton well before dawn on July 21, 2010. Their early start was a defense against lightning, usually not a great danger until afternoon, the normal time for summer storms to gather around the Rocky Mountains.

When they awoke from their somnambulism, they were high on the peak. They saw only blue sky at 9:00 a.m. By 10:00 a.m. gathering morning clouds that historically carried more water than the normal afternoon versions should have signaled serious danger from an earlier-than-normal storm. Two groups were still striving toward the summit at 11:00 a.m., while one group retreated from water droplets crashing into each other, generating lightning.

Around noon National Park Service personnel began receiving cell-phone calls from all three groups of climbers, each struck by lightning on Grand Teton. None of the calls were completely coherent; all were desperate. NPS was fairly certain that one climber was dead. Climbing rangers rallied to keep the total from increasing.

A helicopter returned from fighting forest fires. The Grand hid in clouds when rescuers boarded the helicopter to liftoff from the valley floor, for a Lower Saddle destination where they would coordinate rescues. A local meteorologist took up an observation position to radio advice. The local hospital in Jackson prepared to receive victims, a half-hour ambulance ride

Clouds descend on Grand Teton to hurl lightning at three climbing teams.

from the helicopter landing pad. Dazed victims on the peak tried to determine which way was up and go the other way.

The highest group of climbers had been just 100 vertical feet below the 13,720-foot summit when thunder boomed in the dark clouds that had quickly surrounded them. They piled all metal objects they remembered they were carrying. A low buzzing, later described as sounding like a swarm of bees, caused them to stand as far apart from each other as they could on the narrow ridge they had climbed toward the summit. (Just how many of these climbers ever actually had heard a swarm of bees was a question that would not help to rescue them.) Hoping for insulation, they perched on their climbing ropes and watched their pile of metal possessions and climbing gear pop, vibrate, and spark.

When the bolt struck, all the climbers were knocked to the ground either from the concussion or from electricity coursing through their bodies, causing extreme pain. One was briefly stunned and regained consciousness to the smell of her scorched jacket, hair, and flesh. The climbers looked at each other as their pain eased a bit along with their fear. Then in rain they heard the buzzing resume.

For ninety minutes, strike after strike snapped against the Grand. The strongest strikes were at 12:05 and 12:09 p.m.

The second party of climbers had decided around 11:30 a.m. that the weather had become too scary to proceed. They had begun to rappel (a relatively quick sliding descent on their ropes) when the first very powerful bolt hit, numbing the legs of one of the climbers. Another was reclimbing up the rappel rope to aid the immobilized climber when the second lightning bolt boomed, showering him with gravel and knocking him unconscious even before he could hear the instant thunder. When he came to, he was hanging upside down on the rope, unsure of where he was or which direction was up. Eventually he became reoriented and realized that both of his legs and one arm were useless. With only one arm, he was able to feed rope through his rappelling device and proceed down to try to reach a ledge where he could disconnect from the rope. About five minutes after the first disorienting strike, another bolt pelted him with more small rocks.

Above, his climbing partners were trying to survive. One fell unconscious, bleeding, and not breathing next to another, who could move neither his legs nor arms. Nonetheless, the still-conscious climber managed to give mouth-to-mouth respiration to his friend, which got him breathing again, but mentally confused.

Other members of the party were deaf. Those that still could hear agreed that one of them would try to descend alone to get help.

The group farthest down, ironically led by brothers named Spark, began their retreat after the first big bolt hit. One brother descended a rope to a ledge, ready to aid the least-experienced climber down next. Both made it successfully to the ledge.

Then the second big bolt hit, which not only buckled their legs but slammed them with the force of air expanding from the lightning heat. The jolt threw the less-experienced climber off the ledge. Somehow, later investigation revealed, unsure just how, the falling climber was unattached to his rope protection. The initial fall was eight hundred feet, and the body finally came to rest two thousand feet below.

With only one hand that barely worked, a climber in one of the three groups fumbled a cellphone from his pack and called through a split lip for help. In confusion, he reached his daughter-in-law, but with poor cell coverage he was afraid of the call being dropped. Her call was relayed to the Jenny Lake Climbing Rangers, reaching them at 12:24 p.m.

Famous for their rescues of climbers on the alluring Tetons, even the climbing rangers were confused as subsequent cellphone calls came from the three climbing parties. Were all the calls from the same or different parties? How many total climbers were there? (Eventually they decided sixteen alive, one dead.)

Before the rescue rangers even figured out what they needed to do, two were up in a helicopter headed for the Lower Saddle on Grand Teton. The search and rescue effort began even though rain and thunder made the flight less than secure. It was clear, at least, that precipitation would be snow or hail in the thin, high-altitude air that made gaining lift from the rotor blades difficult as the helicopter raced into dark clouds that masked the Grand.

They knew that if they could find the climbers, the injured would have to be evacuated individually by using a line dangling from the chopper's open door. There was no place for a helicopter to land. A rescue ranger would have to descend the rope to climbers needing rescue, administer first aid, and attach a casualty in either a litter or a full-body sling to the line to be lifted away. (They call the technique a "short-haul," which sounds simpler than it really is, demanding practice by the rescuers before the sadly inevitable need to rescue arrives.) The helicopter pilot had to hold his bird steady in the storm, and the rangers had to clip the victims with exact certainty lest they kill them. For the rescued, if not in terrible shape physically and mentally, the experience could be exhilarating. Of course, all this had to be done in the remaining daylight, or some of the rescued would spend a miserable night with rangers on the mountain.

The helicopter first landed at the Lower Saddle, base camp for the typical ascent of the Grand. There the first two rescue rangers alighted to climb the South Face to search for the injured. On the Lower Saddle, they encountered a professional climbing guide whom they recruited for the mission. Climbing at once, the three rescuers met several climbers making their way down. One ranger stayed with them while the other two rescuers continued up. Fortunately, they saw three more climbers confusedly headed for an attempted descent of a cliff several thousand feet high on the West Face. The rescuers yelled "Death trap!" into the wind. The three climbers heard them and altered their descent to the correct route.

Meanwhile, the storm diminished a bit. The helicopter pilot used the lull to search the routes to the summit. He located all the battered climbers, but it would be an hour before the rescuers could climb to them to start the short-haul evacuation. Another helicopter arrived at the Lower Saddle, carrying more rangers who also began to climb.

The two rescuers from the first helicopter reached the remaining climbers from the lowest group and escorted them down to the Lower Saddle. As is often the case with survivors of lightning strikes, they were mentally as well as physically assaulted. Blue with cold despite warm apparel, streaked with blood, and less than alert, they needed the rescuers' escort.

Once they got this group to safety at the Lower Saddle, the rangers began to ascend again. Aside from the normal challenges of the South Face, they had to climb through temporary waterfalls, up granite slickened by snow, sleet, and rain. When they finally reached the uppermost group of climbers, they gathered them under an overhanging rock and huddled with them to await a short-haul via helicopter. As one of the rescuers stretched a tarp over the rock for extra shelter from renewed precipitation, lightning snapped at his elbow. Everyone removed metal from their vicinity, the climbers growing depressed again after initial encouragement when the helicopter passed above and the rangers arrived. One of the rangers took on the role of comedian and elevated their spirits.

As the storm grew stronger, the light grew dimmer as the end of the day approached. The chopper pilot maneuvered his craft above the rock and tried to hold it steady while the short-haul cable and its rescue attachments were dropped to the rangers. Wind and rain assaulted the pilot's face while his copilot kept watch to make sure the tail rotor was not swinging toward the cliff and a truly newsworthy disaster. The helicopter had proven its capacity to maintain lift in the thin air, but it was pilot skill that kept it steady.

Some two hours later, all but one of the climbers had been evacuated down to the relative safety of the Lower Saddle. There they were transferred to the second chopper for evacuation to medical care on the valley floor. The ever-watchful weatherman was predicting another storm cell and warned that the final short-haul should be postponed, extremely bad news for the final victim even though two rangers would stay with him through the night.

However, within an hour, the helicopter pilot found another short window of flyable weather and yanked the final climber to the Lower Saddle. Fifteen minutes in the shelter wrapped in a sleeping bag and drinking hot chocolate readied him for a quick ride to the valley. He still could not walk, but he had recovered enough feeling to know that he would hike again. Soon he was hooked to an IV line and traveling in an ambulance to Jackson's hospital.

The next day the helicopter pilot headed out again, carrying rangers to recover the body of the climber blasted from the peak by lightning. They could hope that the lightning had killed him before the end of the two-thousand-foot fall. Absent the pilot's flying skill, several other climbers might have died the previous day had the helicopter not been able to rescue them quickly. Approximately ninety rescuers took part in saving sixteen climbers from fearfully fierce lightning.

Some of the survivors experienced reduced hearing. A climber in the highest group had been struck several times and had third-degree burns all over her body, but she was able to walk from the helicopter to the ambulance. At the hospital, she learned that the lightning had exited her body through the index finger of her right hand, damaging the finger so badly that the digit had to be amputated. She had forgotten in the emergency to remove a cheap watch from her wrist while ditching her other metal objects, and the watch had buried its way deep into her wrist. Her left arm was so swollen that physicians had to cut away some of her flesh to get blood flowing to her left hand, which they did manage to save.

After months of surgery, rehabilitation, and healing, she was climbing again. From her experience as a hospital patient, she gained insight about patient care and became a registered nurse.

When the hurlyburly's done,
When the battle's lost and won.
—THE SECOND WITCH, IN *MACBETH* BY WILLIAM SHAKESPEARE

ROCKFALL

Notchtop

―――――――――

It is an old story that grows more complex as each teller adds details, but it always ends the same way: A Native American named Falling Rock disappears in the mountains. The Colorado Department of Transportation keeps trying to find him, posting yellow diamond-shaped signs along roads that read "Watch for Falling Rock." Despite its groan-inciting play on words, this story contains more humor than most stories about falling rocks.

Two climbers were anticipating winter fun when they climbed Notchtop Mountain in Rocky Mountain National Park in February 1983. Notchtop is well-named for the very obvious gap which reveals the sky west of the summit. The notch formed when water freezing in cracks in the granite at the top of the mountain expanded repeatedly over millennia, wedging off chunks or bits of rock less solid than the surrounding rock.

Of course, this meteorological sculpture continues today, sending rock debris to accumulate in piles below the notch. Much more debris, technically called talus, pauses on its way to the bottom of the cliffs, accumulating in a gully often used by climbers for the descent from Notchtop. This loose rock is very unstable beneath climbers' boots, which can cause falling or being hit by rocks being added by gravity to the accumulation.

Neither of the winter climbers wore a helmet, a standard piece of gear for most rock climbers today. Perhaps they were more concerned with hazards that seemed more likely, such as having frostbite reshape their ears or plunging a long distance when loose rock shifted underfoot.

By chance, however, on that winter day, falling rocks were the worst hazard. A barrage hit them as they descended the gully. One climber died instantly from a crushing head wound. The other, also seriously hurt, attempted to reach the trailhead at Bear Lake.

They had told others of their Saturday climbing destination, and on Sunday the National Park Service received word of the climbers' failure to return. Two rangers immediately set out to search for the missing pair, and found the climbers' car parked at Bear Lake. NPS was now faced with a search and rescue mission.

The weather had changed to high wind, invisibility due to blowing snow, and wind chill well below zero. Nevertheless, the two rangers were rugged and experienced enough to guess accurately where to look for the missing climbers. Within a few hours, they found tiny, frozen, red globs of blood at the base of the descent gully on the west flank of Notchtop. Wind had scoured these bits from the accident site and whipped them down the gully. This was not encouraging.

Ascending the gully that was a thoroughfare for deadly rocks, the rangers climbed beyond a bulge of ice and found the first fatality. The dead climber was fastened to one end of a climbing rope; the other end held an empty climbing harness. Fresh rockfall was scattered on the snow,

Notchtop glistens in winter.

indicating that the climbers had been hit by falling rock rather than falling themselves. Despite erasure by the wind, the searchers perceived faint tracks leading down from the death site. The other climber was gone.

Additional rangers had joined the search together with volunteers from a local climbing school, Larimer County Search and Rescue, and Rocky Mountain Rescue. Facing blizzard hazards, these searchers used the first two rangers' observation of tracks to discover the second climbers' body about a hundred yards east of Lake Helene on the way back to Bear Lake. He had covered about a mile, and evidently had died of cold and his head injuries.

The second climber's corpse was hauled from the Lake Helene area back to the trailhead. Blowing snow on Sunday afternoon and Monday delayed removing his climbing partner's body from the steep terrain until Tuesday.

Grand Rockfall

———

In times of error or bad luck, rock climbers can look to Psalm 96 for comfort:

> *God is our refuge and our strength,*
> *a very present help in trouble.*
> *Therefore, we will not fear though the earth be removed,*
> *And the mountains be carried into the midst of the sea.*

Earth removed from mountains often takes the form of falling rocks beginning their journey to the midst of the sea. For a falling rock the size of a volleyball to miss a climber's head in August 1967 and smash his leg into a compound fracture, therefore, was not unusual. But his rescue was.

A National Park Service ranger in Wyoming's Grand Teton National Park, even after an hour of trying, could not talk two climbers out of attempting to ascend the North Face of the 13,770-foot Grand Teton. At that time, this face had not been climbed often because it was so much more precipitous than the South Face. These two climbers, male and female, were both from the University of Illinois and had decided to climb the North Face together.

Of course, they had met before making this decision.

They had seen photos of the very famous and distinctive Grand Teton. The first had been taken in 1872 by pioneer photographer William Henry Jackson, who had to skillfully juggle chemicals in a tent as part of a complicated wet plate process. Success required some luck as well as diligent practice. Jackson had been lucky enough in 1863 to escape death, unlike 51,000 other men who came together with him at the Battle of Gettysburg.

Another Jackson, a fur trapper named David, also had been lucky enough in the 1830s to wander up a valley in which there were no Blackfeet warriors to slay him. Jackson Lake and Jackson Hole east of the base of the Teton Range were named for him. ("Hole" was a fur trappers' term for unforested valley floors.)

The ancestors of the Blackfeet arrived in the vicinity of the valley later called Jackson Hole many generations after their ancestors decided not to endure ice ages in Asia and followed prey across the Bering Land Bridge, which dried out periodically when successive continental glaciers sucked enough water from the oceans to lower sea level. The most recent glaciers, however, did not extend much beyond the high peaks. These icy sculptors that put the finishing touches on the range formed in medieval times, perhaps when bubonic plague killed enough of Europe's population to allow regrowth of forests.

Regrowth of trees that humans had cut down over thousands of years reduced the amount of carbon dioxide in the atmosphere as part of the photosynthetic process in leaves. Reduction of carbon dioxide lessened the greenhouse effect that previously had reduced the reflection of solar heat back into space. Thus, more snow blanketed the Tetons in winter than melted in summer, adding enough weight to high ice fields to cause them to flow down from rock bowls among the peaks into the valley. Flowing ice defines glaciers.

Prevailing wind from the west (due to earth rotation) had dropped snowflakes for millions of years prior to the medieval Little Ice Age, roughing out the peaks and valley with massive glaciers. These glaciers carved the Teton scenery that is so appealing today.

The massive rock block that the glaciers carved rose some sixty million years ago under pressure caused by continental drift smashing together the Pacific and North American plates. The pressure at the plate margins caused buckling of a series of mountain ranges extending east to the Rocky Mountains. These plates floated on the molten rock heated by radio activity and swirling in convection currents far below the earth's surface.

Very near the top of the Grand Teton block some two and a half billion years before its present uplift by continental drift, molten rock at one thousand degrees Fahrenheit squeezed near to the earth's surface and cooled to form granite. A piece of granite of seemingly insignificant size would be broken from the mass by subsequent freezing and thawing, uplift of the Grand, down-dropping of Jackson Hole, and even by the tread of human boots.

"In the beginning," the geologist writing Genesis 1:1 explained, "God created the heavens and the earth."

If any of these events, great and less great, together with innumerable other events had occurred at only a slightly different time, a chunk of granite would not have plummeted about 3:00 p.m. from the North Face of the Grand Teton to smash a climber's leg. Either it would have missed him entirely or it would have pulverized his head. In either case, National Park Service rangers would not have needed to search for a way to achieve a rescue of historically difficult magnitude.

The badly injured male climber fell some twenty feet to a ledge about the size of a dining room table. Twenty feet was a significant drop onto rock, but a lucky distance compared to the alternative of eighteen hundred feet. Both of the climbers yelled for help until they gasped for oxygen in the thin air some twelve thousand feet higher than the oxygen-rich air they were accustomed to breathing in Illinois.

Naturally, the male climber was in more desperate danger than his female colleague. They yelled into wilderness for the remaining afternoon, all the following night, and a seemingly endless number of hours the following day. No one was present to hear them. That is why it is called wilderness.

At first light the day after the rock smashing, the ranger who had discouraged the climb struggled to immobilize a telescope which increased by sixty times each tiny movement. He intended this huge enlargement to pick out on the North Face of the Grand the climbers who had not heeded him. At last, he was able to see two human figures, one unmoving, on a ledge. The search and rescue had begun.

Before noon, two rangers were in a helicopter to search for a rescue plan on the North Face. One of the rangers was among the few climbers who had scaled this route on the Grand. He had fourteen years of climbing experience and eight rescue seasons in the national park. The other ranger was a veteran climber, staring through the helicopter's Plexiglas bubble for a rescue route.

By chance, two other rangers reached the top of the Grand around noon, having enjoyed a climb via the South Face, unaware of the crisis on the North. As they started back down, faint cries alerted them to trouble. Looking over the edge of the North Face, they dimly saw the two stranded climbers about nine hundred feet below.

Soon the recreating rangers heard the helicopter trying to work its way up cliffs that threatened a fatal crash for the pilot and the two ranger passengers. The rangers in the chopper also picked out the victims on a ledge where they had been for nineteen hours. The female climber had been shouting "Help!" for all that time; the male bordered on unconsciousness from loss of blood and extreme pain.

Both climbers thought the helicopter was a tourist ride rather than a search and rescue team. They then realized a ranger in the helicopter was trying to make himself heard with a bullhorn over the chopper's racket. Help was coming.

The helicopter and its pilot had been taken from firefighting duties in nearby Shoshone National Forest, and soon began ferrying nine rangers to the Lower Saddle on the South Face. Assembled in this rescue crew by 4:00 p.m. were the first two helicopter passengers, the ranger who had warned the climbers, the two rangers who descended from the summit, and other experienced rescuers.

They were able to get two of their team to the accident site, traversing fourteen hundred feet across ice and rock left crumbly by millions of attacking freezes and thaws. In three hours, the two rangers extracted the female climber to the relative safety of the Upper Saddle, where other rangers waited to get her off the mountain.

The two rangers at the falling rock site also splinted the male climber's leg as the first day of the rescue grayed toward night. Far below, another team of rescuers led by the park's district ranger moved into position on a glacier to receive the climber they hoped would be lowered eighteen

The North Face of the Grand Teton (on the right) presents greater hazards to climbers than the less sheer South Face.

hundred feet to where they could move him to the nearest point where a helicopter could land. Above, rangers transported very heavy and clumsy loads of ropes, a litter, and two three-hundred-foot steel cables to their fellow rescuers and their badly injured charge. Sleeping bags and most food and water were sacrificed from the load; it was a long, cold night for rangers and victim.

The district ranger radioed for a more powerful helicopter, morphine, more men, and more equipment. By 7:00 the next morning, the district ranger was hovering in a helicopter above the rescue team tending the battered climber. His immediate goal was to throw morphine to one of his rescue rangers on the ledge. Almost miraculously for a man with no ambition to become a major-league outfielder, the district ranger landed the drug in the lap of a rescuer on the ledge.

With the victim sufficiently drugged not to die of shock on the way down, the rescue team had to secure him in the wire litter and lower him eighteen hundred feet, a distance certainly never attempted previously in the national park and likely nowhere else in the Americas. A ranger, of course, had to accompany the victim to prevent the litter from tipping or from crashing into the mountainside.

About five hundred feet down, the victim grew confused and contrary. He demanded to go up, not down. Perhaps pain, loss of blood, and the morphine were having unwelcome side effects. The descending ranger ignored the protests.

With thirteen hundred feet farther to the glacier, a rescuer dropped a rock past the litter to time its fall and thus judge its distance to a ledge ironically called Broadway. Broadway was about halfway down and critical to the next stage of rescue. Another ranger rappelled to Broadway to confirm its distance as three hundred feet lower than the litter. Using only his body for the rappel on two 150-foot ropes tied together, he confirmed a good guess, only a foot short of the shelf. When another ranger followed in the same fashion, friction from the rope left burns on his hip. Another ranger spidered his way down to replace the exhausted rescuer accompanying the litter. It was a strong and competent team.

Night found the group spread along four hundred vertical feet, tired, hungry, and facing another eight hundred feet of descent the next day. They tied themselves into the rock where they could, singly and paired. Rocks screaming past them during the night did not contribute to their rest.

By noon of the third day, the descent team had lowered the victim another five hundred feet in two stretches. They knew they were going to succeed.

The team at the cliff base took over the litter to carry it across the glacier. The helicopter pilot calculated that he could land a little closer than originally planned in a narrow, dead-end canyon. In June of the following year, awards of valor and letters of thanks were passed out for a miraculous rescue.

LOST

Blind Search for Self-Rescue

In 1903, not many people envied Enos Mills his job as Colorado State Snow Observer. His duty was to venture across the state's high mountains in an era before an abundance of high-altitude roads in order to measure snow depths. He decided for himself whether to carry out these journeys on wooden snowshoes (seven pounds) or wooden skis (nine pounds). Snow information was needed to guess the amount of water that would be available in warm months for irrigation, drinking, bathing, washing, recreating, and flushing. If there was not enough water for all these uses in what federal explorer Stephen Long in 1820 labeled the Great American Desert, it was Enos Mills who delivered the bad news.

Mills, of course, did not interpret his duties in this fashion. He was entranced by the opportunity to slog through hundreds of difficult miles, enjoying the glory of snow-covered peaks against cobalt skies, of snow-clothed evergreen trees, and of the weasels, hares, and small alpine grouse called white-tailed ptarmigan that all turned white to survive the winter.

Although Mills certainly was aware of hazards to winter survival, he seemed either very courageous or very oblivious about such dangers. Frostbite to ears, cheeks, nose, fingers, and toes was almost assured at high altitude where wind frequently roared at more than a hundred miles per hour and there was no campfire fuel or shelter. Such high winds usually lifted snow to form cornices above cliffs with no support below. An unwary admirer of the view into a valley could venture onto a cornice and cause it to collapse under the extra weight, sending him into a fall of hundreds or thousands of feet. If the snow observer was looking up from a valley when a cornice collapsed for no apparent reason, the resulting avalanche might

A white-tailed ptarmigan in winter camouflage grazes among tree line shrubs.

be the last snow he would ever observe. Water managers on the plains would have to get along without his report. Yet Mills was delighted to get paid to be able to experience the high-mountain winter wonders.

Another risk of which Mills was aware, at least insofar as its results, was exposure to very high doses of ultraviolet radiation. The thin air at high altitude provided much less natural shielding from UV rays, and this radiation nearly doubled when it reflected off snow. Mills did smear ashes on his exposed skin to lessen sunburn, a substance unlikely to be found in modern sunscreens but nonetheless effective. Of course, he could not smear ashes into his eyes, which he shielded with darkened glasses or goggles, similar to today's sunglasses.

After a heavy snowstorm dumped fresh powder on the high peaks and the clouds cleared to blue sky, Mills began a typical trudge, snowshoeing from the west side of the Rockies through the subalpine vegetative zone where the most snow collected. In the dense forest watered in summer by its reservoirs of snow, a mature Engelmann spruce had accumulated a shaky mass of white. As warming temperatures destabilized its load, the entire mass dumped onto Mills. An arborial avalanche surely was nothing new for him, but this time it swept what he called "snow glasses" from his face and buried them out of sight.

Unable to find his glasses and unwilling to turn back due to lack of eye protection, Mills continued climbing. Except when watching a bird build its nest or a beaver its dam or when watching a bear gorge on berries, he was never accused of being patient.

In any case, such aggravation disappeared when he climbed above the forest's protective shade. At tree line he met a flock of white-tailed ptarmigan feeding on the new-growth twigs of alpine willows. In summer, when the feathers on these small grouse perfectly camouflaged them as rocks protruding from alpine tundra, Mills had likely been startled at somewhat higher elevation when a rock flew from underneath his descending boot. The surprise multiplied if it was actually a hen followed by a group of newly fledged chicks. Many mountaineers had their hearts pushed from their throats and then grinned after such a ptarmigan experience.

But to see these grouse whose summer plumes had molted into white feathers that camouflaged them to resemble the thousands of snow-covered rocks at the lowest part of their range was a rare treat even for someone with Mills's vast wildlife photo opportunity experience. He pulled a bulky camera from his pack and began photographing the flock, typically tame in their perfect camouflage. Mills wore a hat to shade his eyes from UV radiation pouring from blue skies, but for a half hour the snow hiding the ptarmigan from even the eyes of soaring golden eagles was reflecting UV radiation into his bare eyes.

Mills mentioned in writings about his winter experiences that other Colorado folks told him such journeys were less than wise, but he lived according to his own priorities. Interacting with the glory of the mountains was his highest priority. Comfort, food, and safety he relegated down the list. He often reported running out of the small ration (typically a pocket of raisins) he carried. He never reported running out of film.

Soon after he finally managed to pull himself away from photographing ptarmigan, Mills felt his eyelids begin to adhere to his eyes. Sharp pain followed, and then blindness. He had to find his way down the mountains to help while sightless. There were no rangers to rescue him. No search and rescue team would set out to find him. No one knew where he was.

He carried a ten-foot walking staff, which assisted in calculating snow depth for the state's water managers. He had been climbing from west to east and believed that he would find potential aid closer on the east slope. He continued in the direction he had been heading, over the mountain pass and down the other side.

Mills's staff served as a poor substitute for his eyes as he felt his way down the east side of the mountain. He took careful steps to avoid falling off a cliff. Hoping that his waving staff would hit a tree, he took at least twice as long to descend to the tree line and potential fuel for a warming fire as he would have taken had he been able to see. (He had grabbed a hatchet and his camera in his post-blizzard haste to reach the heights, but he had forgotten or ignored food.)

After he at last reached tree line, he tried to find a route marked down the east slope by feeling for blazes cut in bark. The fresh snow covered the blazes, forcing him to dig down through the snow in attempting to find them. This route-searching technique surely added pain to his frigid fingers to supplement the agony in his eyes. Eventually he could feel no more blazes because there were none as he realized that he had almost walked off a cliff.

Although he had felt some blazes, Mills was losing confidence that he was headed east toward aid rather than retracing his ascent route to the west. As he retreated from the cliff, he noticed cooling temperature that indicated the approaching end to a short winter day. He worked his way down a forested slope, planning to reach the floor of the canyon into which he almost had fallen and follow the watercourse at the bottom toward rescue.

On the way, he shouted often in hopes of attracting sighted rescue. His only responses were echoes, which did give him some notion about the shape of the surrounding landscape.

If he was headed east, Mills knew that most of the trees would be limber pines, which typically grow on south-facing slopes. On north-facing slopes, Engelmann spruce predominate. He was reassured to feel that the trees amid which he snowshoed had the limber pines' semi-long, soft needles growing in bundles of five. Engelmann spruce have short, stiff and sharp needles, growing individually along their branches and twigs. He was headed east.

He further attempted to verify his assumption by digging into the snow and removing his wet mittens to feel rocks that he believed would have more lichens growing on the north than on the south side. He remembered the old belief that more moss grows on the north side of trees than on the south. Mills, of course, knew the difference, as many do not, between moss and lichens. With at least a thousand years of undisturbed growth available to them, the lichens had plenty of time to cover the whole rock, with no difference in density discernible by his frigid fingers. The theory was based on the north side of rocks or trees being shadier, hence less subject to drying by evaporation and encouraging more lichen or moss growth. Mills also checked trees and decided that this method did nothing to confirm his direction of travel, about which he already was confident.

After several hours of very slow descent (cold was a factor, even if darkness meant nothing), Mills reached the canyon floor and heard a stream flowing below ice, but the floor was choked with fallen trees and large rocks fallen from surrounding cliffs, making progress even more difficult. Moreover, he thought the bottom of the canyon might contain a drop-off, blocking his route to rescue.

Mills therefore decided to climb back up the canyon wall to continue descending along the edge. This did not work because the wall was too steep. He found and followed a narrow ledge, but a snow cornice extended from the edge. When he walked on the cornice, it collapsed beneath his weight, dumping him onto a lower snow-covered ledge.

Fearing another fall, Mills tried to climb down from the ledge. Swinging his staff, he found a dead tree leaning against the ledge from below. Breaking off dead branches, he threw them down the cliff to determine how high he was. He guessed from the time it took to hear them hit the canyon floor that he was about thirty feet up the wall. He threw his staff after the branches and, still wearing his snowshoes, began to shinny down the limbless tree. When he arrived on the ground, he felt for his staff and continued down the canyon.

As he descended, the floor became less clogged where the canyon widened. Mills paused to yell to judge what the echoes told him about his surroundings, but before he could shout, he heard newly fallen snow crashing in an avalanche from his right. Blind, he had no idea where it would hit—in front, behind, or on top of him. He could hear rocks and trees crashing together in the falling mass. It plunged to the canyon floor so closely in front of him that the rush of air pushed out of the avalanche path knocked him over.

Swirling clouds of snow and rock dust covered him. When the tumult faded, he walked on. A dozen snowshoe steps further, he encountered the wreckage of snow, dirt, rocks, and uprooted, smashed trees. He tried to feel his way around it, but three or four hundred feet wide, the debris filled the canyon from wall to wall to a height of about sixty feet, as he discovered when he had to climb over it.

When Mills made his first attempt to climb the debris, it gave way, dropping him into a pond that was forming behind the new dam of avalanche rubble. His ten-foot staff caught on the debris and prevented him from sinking above his hips. He still had his snowshoes on, and they snagged on the shattered ice, holding his lower body in the water. As he tried to free himself, a large mass of snow fell on him, nearly causing him to lose his grip on the staff. Finally, he extricated himself and pulled his body onto the debris mass. For the first time, he was scared.

Because his snowshoes would not help him climb over the debris wall, Mills took them off to carry under his arm. As he descended the other side, the debris under his feet collapsed. He fell, losing one snowshoe. For an hour he felt around and dug through snow without finding it. He estimated that the temperature was about zero. His feet, no longer held above the snow, were nearly frozen.

Mills then found a dead bighorn sheep ram killed by the avalanche. He warmed his hands on the newly killed ram and began to philosophize about how the fit animal had died while he, though blind, had survived. He surmised that a star-filled sky shown above the path of the slide, which ascended to the sky. He then decided he should find that lost snowshoe. He did.

His wet pants froze as he snowshoed down the canyon. He stopped to make a fire of dead branches gathered in the cold dark. The heat of the flames caused greater pain in his eyes, forcing him to continue downstream before he was completely dry.

Often as he strode through the night, too active to succumb to hypothermia, Mills stopped to apply snow to try to relieve the burning in his eyes. He noted that most of the trees among which he passed were sharp-needled Engelmann spruce mixed with soft-needled subalpine fir and a few limber pines. Soon after the futile drying at his campfire, he reached a broad area burned by forest fire where no needles remained on the dead trees.

While applying snow to his eyes, he heard owls hooting in the open area, indicative of spring, the time of heaviest snow in the Rockies. He also came upon a flock of mountain chickadees roosting in an abandoned woodpecker hole a short way above his head. Disturbed by Mills, they flew out of their hole, shrilling a burry *chick-a-dee-dee-dee*. He regretted disturbing them.

As the sun rose, the light caused Mills's eyes increased pain. Resting on the snow, he smelled fragrant aspen smoke, evidently hinting potential rescue. He shouted but received no response. He guessed that loss of sight had bolstered his sense of smell. The aspen smoke would have originated in a stove two or three miles distant. He rose to search for its source.

Mills enjoyed remembering the previous day's beauty before snow had taken his vision. He heard birds sing and icicles fall. The smell of aspen smoke grew stronger. When he felt he was in the shadow of passing clouds, he tried to guess their size and shape by how long it took them to pass.

At mid-afternoon, Mills smelled old horse manure, and then his waving staff hit a cabin corner. He shouted for its inhabitants but heard no answer. Feeling his way around the cabin, he found a door barred by a board nailed across it. He ripped off the board, entered the cabin, and found a stove and wood. He started a fire and dropped snow on the stove to form steam to try to relieve his eyes' pain. This seemed to help. He sat on the floor near the stove and fell asleep leaning against a wall. Of course, the fire burned out, and when Mills awoke, he was too cold to rise.

He was grateful that he had still been wearing his mittens or his fingers would have frozen. By rubbing himself, he finally was warmed and limbered enough to rise and build another fire. An hour later, he stopped shivering in the rewarmed room. Sixty hours after he'd last eaten, he realized he was hungry and managed to find a few raisins that had resided unnoticed in a pocket. Feeling around the cabin, he failed to find any other food.

Mills fell asleep again and woke at what he guessed was noon. He tried steaming again to relieve his eyes.

Going to the door, he listened to a nearby gray jay. Then he heard a Steller's jay. The gray jay landed on his shoulder, looking for a handout. Mills tried to explain to the jays that he had no food. He speculated that the prospector who had lived in the cabin had made friends with the birds. Mills wished that he might become acquainted with this fellow bird lover.

Again Mills smelled aspen smoke. Again he shouted. Again there was no response.

He tried to decide if he should stay in the cabin or feel his way along the road that surely led to it. Meanwhile, he heard the open water of a stream and then the singing of a water ouzel. The ouzel's hopeful song inspired Mills to continue his blind progress. He wrote an explanatory note to the cabin's owner and snowshoed along a road through the woods. A side road to an abandoned prospect hole caused him to lose his way, but he backtracked to the main road.

When the road widened into a broad space, the smell of aspen smoke grew much stronger. Mills knew his blind search for rescue from the summit had succeeded. He feared passing his safety and stood still listening. He then heard the voice of rescue. A small girl asked, "Are you going to stay here tonight?"

Enos Mills recovered his sight, but on a hike over the same route the following summer, he did not see his missing snow glasses. More than a century later, the lenses of those glasses lie on the forest floor, buried under needles of the still-standing spruce that snatched them. There are many under which to look.

Missing Mom

———

There is a mountain in the distant West
That, sun-defying, in its deep ravines
Displays a cross of snow on its side.
Such is the cross I wear upon my breast
These eighteen years, through all the changing scenes
And seasons, changeless since the day she died.
—HENRY WADSWORTH LONGFELLOW, IN *A CROSS OF SNOW*,
WRITTEN EIGHTEEN YEARS AFTER HIS WIFE DIED IN A HOUSE FIRE

Since William Henry Jackson hauled an 11-by-14 wet plate camera up Colorado's Notch Mountain in 1873 to make the first photo of Mount of the Holy Cross, the 14,005-foot peak has been the world's most easily recognized mountain. An image of its northeast face has even appeared on a United States postage stamp. Intersecting snow-filled gullies forming a natural Christian emblem 1,400 feet tall and 750 feet wide have inspired poets, photographers, and painters and attracted uncounted mountain climbers.

Subsequent falling of rocks supporting much of the right side of the cross has not prevented public eagerness to approach the mountain for a close view or to reach the summit. Because it is just barely more than fourteen thousand feet high among Colorado's more than fifty "fourteeners," Holy Cross also attracts climbers seeking to ascend many, if not all, of this famous collection.

Although a long and tiring haul, Mount of the Holy Cross is not as technically difficult to ascend as some other fourteeners. Its ascent does not inevitably expose climbers to long falls, as does Longs Peak. The rock on Holy Cross is solid, unlike the brittle, tumble-prone surface of the Maroon Bells. On the other hand, no one drives to the top of Holy Cross as they can on the fourteeners Pikes Peak and Mount Evans.

Unlike the "deadly Bells," alliterative Pikes Peak, Mount Evans, and Longs, Mount of the Holy Cross does not present itself for an easy, close-up view. With its famous snow ravines, Holy Cross hides.

Surrounding peaks do not completely mask it. Holy Cross is clear through good binoculars from the thirteen-thousand-foot Arapahoes in the Indian Peaks Wilderness. A less-than-satisfactory view is available from a turnout on the west end of the Eisenhower Tunnel along Interstate 70. Jackson scouted his first photo of this already legendary peak from the top of another fourteener, fifteen miles to the east, Grays Peak. Shrine Pass, along a delightful wildflower hike, is named for its view of Mount of the Holy Cross.

But for the best view, the classic view, admirers of Mount of the Holy Cross must follow Jackson's 1873 expedition up Notch Mountain in today's Holy Cross Wilderness, administered by the USDA Forest Service. This trek has become a pilgrimage goal, with amenities in surrounding towns and a shelter on Notch Mountain to serve hikers with more devotion than stamina.

Such was not the case, however, in September 2004, with two hikers eagerly anticipating a climb to the summit of Holy Cross. One already had climbed thirty-eight fourteeners. The other was his wife's friend, a marathon runner and mother to four children.

Clearly, neither of these hikers prepared for climbing by watching nature documentaries on television. But the best conditioning for climbing mountains is climbing mountains rather than running along unpaved roads at relatively lower altitude. Conditioning for fourteeners ideally should include ascending a series of successively higher mountains of eleven, twelve, and thirteen thousand feet. Thus, the male climber had packed in a high ratio of red blood cells. The female climber was very fit for conditions several thousand feet lower than Mount of the Holy Cross, but unprepared for higher altitudes. Much of her gear was purchased the

Mount of the Holy Cross was first photographed from Notch Mountain in 1873.

day previous to the climb instead of bearing the scars of instructive use. Such preparation was more optimistic than effective.

Despite joyful discussion and planning, their hike up Mount of the Holy Cross did not go flawlessly. The marathoner started the hike suffering from a headache. Perhaps it was due to altitude, or her kids had brought home some inconspicuous infection from school. Perhaps she needed to have produced more red blood cells to capture more oxygen working hard in the thin mountain air. Perhaps she just had bad luck.

Eventually the male climber discovered he had left a water purification device in the car along with some sandwiches. For each of them to have carried a gallon of water (eight pounds) would not have been too much. The chances of being able to stick the water purifier into a pool or stream above tree line were slight. Moreover, the chances of contracting disease from unpurified water were not 100 percent, and symptoms would occur only after they arrived home. The sandwiches (counter to the protestations of some wilderness survivalists) were not so critical; the climbers did have energy snacks.

Their really big mistake was getting lost. Mount of the Holy Cross has multiple routes favored by various climbers for their preferred advantages leading to the summit. A sign indicating the least difficult North Ridge route was missing because it was being refurbished. Therefore, the two climbers ended up on the more circuitous (scenic) Halo route, normally ascended in two days instead of their projected one. Instead of a topographical map, which more clearly indicates the shape of the land (for those who can read such maps), the two climbers were using a sketch map. A sketch map is much more informative than it sounds and often is favored for its ease of interpretation. When they got around to consulting their map, they did not perceive their route-finding error until they had gone too far to retreat to the intended trail and still have time to reach the summit.

So they pushed on, running out of water by the time they were within a half mile of the top with an elevation gain of only five hundred feet remaining ahead. There the marathoner gave out and told her companion to go on to the top without her. This he was reluctant (reasonably) to do, but ultimately the lure of the summit overcame good sense, a common mountaineering error. When tired from climbing, the mind fails before the body, which can determinedly carry on into disaster.

He told her to traverse, in her exhausted state, across big rocks around the summit to the North Ridge Trail, by which they had intended to ascend and which is the descent route for nearly all Holy Cross climbers. Neither of them could see the North Ridge Trail, which was actually much farther away than the six hundred feet he estimated. Neither had any idea if they would encounter each other prior to reaching the trailhead.

No one ever reported seeing her again.

He was on top about twelve minutes later, called his wife, talked briefly with other climbers, exchanged cameras for mutual commemorative summit photos, and was off after five minutes. He shouted for his companion all the way down. No reply. Hours later, she was not at the trailhead.

Some search and rescue team members set out to find her before dark. By the time a week had passed, more than seven hundred seekers had blanketed the area in the largest search and rescue mission in Colorado history. At times five helicopters buzzed overhead, one equipped with a heat-sensing device. Five canine search teams trotted into the search. They all took hope from the rescue of another woman eight years previously after she was missing for nine days.

Their massive effort was fruitless. One dog team found a patch of what looked like blood on a snowbank; whether or not it was human was never determined because heavy rain washed it away before further examination. There were no tracks in the snow.

Searchers found a watch hanging on a tree branch, but it did not belong to the missing woman. More ominously, they found a shotgun abandoned in a duffel bag below tree line a short way from a trail. The firearm could not be connected with its owner.

A search team found an individual zipped into his tent who refused to show himself or answer questions. Another search team encountered a backpacker who hid behind a tree, concealing his face, and then ran down the mountain. A search team led by sheriff's deputies questioned a lone backpacker who only reluctantly gave a name but was carrying no identification to verify it, and he was vague about where he lived. At the time, none of these encounters received much attention because searchers assumed they were looking for an accident victim. When a monthlong criminal investigation eventually began following the abandonment of the search, these suspicious happenings were too long past to be examined more closely.

As the last person to see the marathoner alive, her climbing companion was questioned closely. The marathoner's husband denied definitely that the two climbers were jointly involved in any activity other than mountaineering or that the male climber would ever harm the marathoner. The husband did decry the disastrous decision to leave his wife below the summit.

Looking at Mount of the Holy Cross from William Henry Jackson's first photo viewpoint on Notch Mountain, pilgrims and climbers think the vista before them is huge and complicated. They can believe that someone could fall or be otherwise initiated into victimhood and never be found.

History, however, indicates that this is not true. When search and rescue fails, accidental discovery by ever-increasing numbers of wilderness recreationalists always turns up accident victims, some many years later, but most within weeks or months. The only exceptions are victims buried under tons of rock and silt by flash floods or under rockslides in the brittle sedimentary rock of the Elk Mountains (Maroon Bells). Searching for remains of the lost marathoner continued from time to time for years after the huge search ended.

Moreover, in the Holy Cross Wilderness dogs accompanying hikers are not required to be leashed if they are reliably responsive to voice commands and do not harass wildlife and if a leash is available in case requirements one and two are not met. Although this practice is uncertain from the standpoint of dog safety, it does greatly increase the chance that some non–search and rescue dog will turn up what the working dogs have failed to find. No dogs have found the marathoner's remains.

Given that Holy Cross climbers face their greatest hazard while driving on Interstate 70 on the way to Half Moon Trailhead, the Holy Cross Wilderness is a safe place. Danger from black bears and mountain lions is infinitesimal. Furthermore, animals never consume boots and hiking poles.

No one is happy with the conclusion that the failure to find the marathoner's remains leaves scant explanation for her disappearance other than murder. Nonetheless, everyone familiar with the case wonders about the searchers' encounter with at least one odd-acting man and about a possible connection to an abandoned shotgun. Did some creepy character initiate a scenario with a solitary and tired woman, perhaps dehydrated and mountain sick, that ended with murder? The idea contaminates the most naturally sanctified spot in the Rocky Mountains.

The marathoner's son, eleven years old at the time of his mother's disappearance, of course reads the extensive speculations online about what might have happened on Mount of the Holy Cross. He has commented via the internet, "We have become a strong family because of this and as we say 'Always remember. Never forget.'"

Maroon Bells

—————

Oh, the bells, bells, bells!
What a tale their terror tells . . .!
—EDGAR ALLAN POE IN *THE BELLS*

The magnificent Maroon Bells are among the Rockies' most popular peaks to photograph. They even appear in a 2018 series of postage stamps called "O Beautiful." Despite their famous beauty, however, the Bells are not particularly attractive to mountaineers because, unlike most other high peaks in Colorado, the Maroon Bells are not rock solid. Climbers have learned not to take them for granite. They are made of sedimentary rock that formed flat until tilted by continental drift with layers trending down, like a house roof.

Moreover, the rock composing the Elk Mountains, of which the Maroon Bells are part, is what climbers, with somewhat extreme dislike, call rotten. It is quite likely to snap off under a booted foot and send a climber falling down the aforementioned downward slant.

On the other hand, they are the Maroon Bells. Their extreme beauty looks to adults like two bells sitting next to each other. To children they look as mountains should, symmetrical in proportion and pointed on top. Of course, the Bells attract understandably eager climbers. The USDA Forest Service, which administers the federal forest from which the Maroon Bells rise, labels them officially as the "Deadly Bells" in hopes of reducing the need for search and rescue missions. Posted beneath maroon mountain majesties, the Forest Service warning may often be overlooked. But the

"Golden bells! What a world of happiness their harmony foretells!" from Edgar Allan Poe's The Bells.

accident rate would be even higher if the Feds neglected to publicize the danger.

On a Forest Service warning sign set where most climbers would see it, the final and thereby most emphatic warning reads, "Expert climbers who did not know the proper routes have died on these peaks."

Such an expert with much backcountry experience drove from northern New Mexico in September 2016. He planned to climb Maroon Peak (14,156 feet), descend 235 feet to a knife-edge ridge, scramble with care along its 2,100 feet, and ascend to the 14,014-foot summit of North Maroon Peak before climbing down to the reflection of yellow aspen in justifiably famous Maroon Lake. His goal for the next day was the 14,018-foot top of Pyramid Peak, equally crumbly and nearby to the east.

During the warm months, the Forest Service closely regulates access to the Bells. Most admirers of their wonder arrive by shuttle bus, which eliminates soul-crushing traffic and lung-clogging pollution in the narrow Maroon Creek valley, walled on both sides by high peaks. This supervision recorded the New Mexico climber entering the valley to approach the three-mile trail to the base of Maroon Peak at 11:00 a.m. It was a late start, but he likely was justifiably confident of reaching his goal quickly. Another climber saw him on Maroon Peak at 1:40 p.m. He made a cellphone call between 4:00 and 6:00 p.m. from either Maroon Peak or North Maroon Peak. (The peaks were too close together for subsequent investigators to identify which summit.) Perhaps he was reporting success to someone.

In any case, a parking lot attendant noted seeing the New Mexico climber the next morning. This sighting fitted with his projected schedule. A map of Pyramid Peak was found in his car, perhaps forgotten. He was not known to carry crampons to strap to his feet to grab fresh snow, although he did have micro spikes intended for a similar purpose on slick surfaces. He was wearing khaki pants and a black long-sleeved shirt, and perhaps a gray jacket. A blue helmet would protect his head from deadly falling rocks. No one saw him again.

When he was reported missing, search and rescue teams and the Pitkin County Sheriff's Office quickly launched a thorough search. They knew the drill. Boots on the ground and search dog teams were encouraged by the sound of multiple helicopters overhead. A fixed-wing aircraft equipped with a million-dollar camera tried to pick up his image. Normally, such sophisticated efforts could at least locate a body. This time, they failed.

Such searches went on for nearly a year, during which time normal hiking activity would be expected to stumble on a body when search and rescue could not. The last major push saw search and rescue teams from as far away as Boulder join Mountain Rescue Aspen, Garfield County Search and Rescue, West Elk Search and Rescue, Alpine Rescue Team from Evergreen, and Vail Mountain Rescue Group. Helicopters inserted human and canine searchers into whatever basin, onto whatever slope where anyone could imagine that a body might be found. Not a clue turned up, and the search was abandoned.

It was time for writers of mystery fiction to wade in. The body was in either a glacier-carved lake or a recent very heavy rockslide, unnoticeable among so many that tear down the Deadly Bells.

Dunes Doom

The initial search and rescue mission was straightforward and quick. When rangers in Colorado's Great Sand Dunes National Park noticed a car parked in a horse trailer unloading area for five days in February 2017, they became concerned. They traced the rented car to a man from Phoenix, New York. The winter weather was cold and snowy, and a search seemed warranted.

Various search and rescue teams joined the National Park Service to locate the car's driver. Alamosa County Search and Rescue, El Paso County Search and Rescue, and the Colorado Division of Fire Prevention and Control gathered for the search. Dogs and aircraft joined the effort. Some twenty-eight searchers participated in locating the lost visitor.

They found him in the afternoon of the first day's search, a mile and a half south of the park headquarters. Evidently he had become disoriented while hiking through the dunes and had wandered for many miles, lost, trying to find his way back to his car. He seemed to be in reasonably good condition despite snowstorms, high winds, and nighttime temperatures in the teens.

The National Park Service was glad they had found him alive and unharmed. They did not speculate how he had gotten lost.

The dunes, of course, have no trails and not many landmarks within the constantly changing hills of sand. On the other hand, the Sangre de Cristo Range, the southernmost range within the Rockies, is obvious, extending around 250 miles from southern Colorado into northern New Mexico. The mountains were given their name, which translates to "Blood of

The Sangre de Cristo Range towers above Great Sand Dunes National Park.

Christ," in 1719 by a Spanish explorer impressed by alpenglow spreading down the high, snowy summits.

Immediately east of the dunes, these mountains rise to 13,604 feet, more than a mile above the hills of sand. They, together with the San Juan Range, a short way to the west, trap the sand deposited by swirling winds. Buttressing the high peaks immediately adjacent to the park are the four-teeners Crestone Peak (14,294 feet) to the north and Blanco Peak (14,345 feet) to the south. The wall of the Sangres is an extremely obvious indicator of direction within the dunes. Moreover, the lost visitor was found and rescued near a highway from which passing traffic should have been audible on occasion. Perhaps winter wind and snow hid these landmarks.

How he could have gotten lost for five days of wandering was puzzling. But at least the search and rescue effort had been comparatively slight and completely successful. Interviewed after his rescue by a Denver television station, the lost park visitor seemed to be in the midst of some midlife crisis. "I was trying to find motivation for the next forty years of my life," he explained. "I wanted to exert myself. I didn't want to go to the extremes I did."

Added to the drifting sand was the barrier of drifting snow. He vowed, "This isn't going to stop me. Three feet isn't going to stop me. Four feet isn't going to stop me. I'm going to keep going. Why? I couldn't tell you."

He returned to Great Sand Dunes in May. Again, rangers noticed his car, parked near a picnic area for several days with no indication of a camping permit or hiking itinerary. When the car was not moved, NPS launched another search and rescue mission six days after the visitor from New York evidently entered the park.

Dog teams came from Larimer, Park, and El Paso Counties. The Division of Fire Prevention showed up with a fixed-wing aircraft, together with USDA Forest Service and Flight for Life helicopters, to join the search teams. The search covered twenty-seven square miles in the national park and the adjacent national preserve. After a week, high winds and snow frustrated search efforts and endangered searchers, and the effort was reduced.

Seven weeks after the search was ended, two hikers who had not been involved discovered the lost hiker's body on a dip in the topography between Milwaukee Peak and Marble Mountain. Custer County Search and Rescue, Saguache County Search and Rescue, and Western Mountain Rescue subsequently recovered the body, which was lifted out by helicopter.

May is winter on top of the Sangres. The lost visitor died of hypothermia more than thirteen thousand feet above sea level.

Recovering a Lost Treasure Hunter

From northern New Mexico to the Canadian border, treasure hunters search for a chest hidden in the Rocky Mountains. Supposedly, it contains approximately $2 million worth of gold, jewels, and even a couple of pieces of pre-Columbian Native American adornment.

Forest Fenn, an art dealer from Santa Fe, has claimed that he hid this treasure as incentive for people to enter the wilds to benefit from getting off couches to enjoy nature. He has published a poem containing clues to the chest's location.

Perhaps a bigger mystery than the chest's whereabouts is why Fenn believes that further incentive beyond natural attraction is needed to encourage exploring the Rocky Mountain wilds. The public enthusiasm for such activity is amply demonstrated by the publisher of the book you are holding, which produces a hundred FalconGuides a year to serve forms of outdoor adventure quite aside from an improbable treasure chest. Moreover, guidebooks increase greatly the likelihood of travelers in untrammeled nature remaining safe. As of this writing, four treasure hunters have died from New Mexico to Wyoming.

Perhaps these deaths are statistically no greater than death that would have occurred from other causes. It can be reasonably argued that the activity Fenn encourages is likely to delay more death than it incites.

Search and rescue teams, however, are inclined to believe that the treasure hunters would be better off reading guidebooks than pondering obscure poetic clues. First in line among these search and rescue skeptics may be the Park County Sheriff's Search and Rescue. They had to rescue the same Virginia treasure hunter three times in four years from the same Wyoming wilds.

Moreover, this perpetually lost soul was from Lynchburg, arguably an even more appealing outdoor environment than the Wyoming wilds where she imagined the treasure chest was hidden. Certainly, Park County search and rescue teams wished she would stay thousands of miles away at home to enjoy her own area's great natural appeal.

Her first attempt, in 2013, in company with a male associate, resulted in a June rescue after they were lost for four days. They were extracted from the Big Creek area west of Cody, suffering from exposure. (June in Wyoming differs significantly from June in Virginia.) High water prevented them from crossing Big Creek, which evidently seemed necessary for treasure-hunting success.

Although most treasure hunters search in the Santa Fe area, some reasonably suppose that Fenn's poetry refers to Wyoming, where he has considerable personal history. As a child, he often vacationed with family in West Yellowstone. In Cody, he was associated with the Buffalo Bill Center of the West. A former Air Force pilot, he enjoyed frequently flying to Billings, Montana, in order to visit the Little Bighorn Battlefield. Therefore, if he was hiding treasure somewhere in the Rockies south of Canada, Park County, Wyoming, was a good guess.

In 2015 the two treasure hunters were stymied in the same area when the woman fell and broke her ankle. She had to be airlifted to medical aid. The predominantly volcanic rock in the area erodes to dramatic spines and towers, and it is likely to cause more such accidents than the granite, schist, and gneiss of the Teton and Wind River Ranges of Wyoming or the southern Rockies.

After the second rescue, the couple was warned not to return until they had learned more about wilderness survival. They were told they risked arrest if found on private land. But such arrest was unlikely given the vast preponderance of public land in Wyoming that is open to everyone.

In 2016 an area resident reported that he had seen a female hiker leaving the Jim Mountain Trailhead on July 15 and that her car remained there on July 18. The car was registered to the same Virginia treasure hunter,

Volcanic rock can break, sending treasure hunters into injury.

maybe accompanied by her searching companion. An aerial search of the area where the pair had been rescued previously ended after two hours. There was no way to guess in which direction they might have walked.

At mid-morning on July 18, the female seeker after treasure emerged from the wilderness unharmed. She had seen the search aircraft but did not attempt to signal it because she did not know it was looking for her. She had seen grizzly bears three times during her treasure hunt and "had had enough." Photos taken by hikers in the Jim Mountain area frequently include huge grizzly tracks.

Ranchers gave her a ride back to her vehicle. She proclaimed she was driving back to Virginia and had no intention of returning to Wyoming.

The head of search and rescue for the Park County Sheriff's Office commented that the search cost was not high because it was conducted by volunteers. The cost of fuel for the search aircraft was about $100. There was no charge to the treasure hunter.

He was not convinced of the Virginian's resolve not to return. He believed that strong conviction about the identity of poetic landmarks was a nearly irresistible draw to seekers of the treasure chest. He expressed the hope that they would add backcountry survival guides to their reading list.

Naturally, no treasure hunter would reveal to any potential search and rescue crew where the search for treasure would lead. Hence, searchers have little idea about where to look for treasure hunters who may be in trouble. "People from the big cities are so used to help being just a phone call away," the search and rescue leader bemoaned. "I think they have financial blinders on, or economic blinders on. They can't see anything but the treasure."

Some other treasure hunters agree with a Wyoming hiding place. Their most recent fatality was not far away, a fall from a five-hundred-foot cliff in Yellowstone National Park.

Fenn points out that the bronze chest is ten by ten inches and five inches deep. It weighs forty-two pounds and has to be where Fenn (eighty years old at the time of hiding) could safely walk. The eventually successful hunter, he claims, should remain safe.

White House Calling

Unsurprisingly, the parents of a sixteen-year-old girl missing in Colorado wilderness thought their daughter's absence was of special concern. To search and rescue teams in Rocky Mountain National Park, the wandering teen was a serious matter but not an unusual one. Then the park received a telephone call: "This is the White House. Please hold for the vice president."

The chief ranger thought it an odd time for a joke. But perhaps the tensions of the second day of an increasingly troublesome search suggested that humor was an appropriate relief. Nearly all of the two-hundred-some search and rescue incidents annually experienced by the national park end happily. Most end quickly with relative simplicity.

On the second day of this particular search in 1995, the situation was becoming more complicated. Although young, the girl was presumed to be in excellent shape, on the staff of a nearby youth camp famous for the quality of its hiking program. She was familiar with the terrain, which contained many peaks higher than thirteen thousand feet above sea level.

Less positively, she was a teenage girl proud of her abilities and challenged by her peers to prove herself. Could she in one day climb a string of six peaks in the Mummy Range? All but one were more than thirteen thousand feet high.

The day appointed for the sixteen-mile escapade involved problematic weather of gusty winds and frozen precipitation typical for August. Nevertheless, her parents, who were visiting from Tennessee, drove her to a 3:30 a.m. start along the one-way, unpaved Fall River Road to the Chapin Pass Trailhead. There was no obvious indication in the darkness (beyond

A summer storm sheathes the Mummy Range in clouds, making a bad day for climbing.

hiking history that the hiker, if not her parents, surely knew) that foul weather was likely to brew in the afternoon. No one would do much hiking in this extremely popular park for pedestrians if they did not accept the risk of bad weather. She was prepared with good gear and an equally good attitude.

The normal predawn chill was a comfort as she followed the initial steep stretch of trail through classically beautiful subalpine forest that she could barely see in the fringe of her flashlight beam. Soon the trail leveled at Chapin Pass. Before it descended on the other side, she cut right, leaving the main trail on a vague path through low-growing ground cover. Avoiding tripping over rocks and bushes, she soon ascended above the tree line.

Escaping the dark confines of thick forest might have made her way easier to see even in the still gloomy blackness. But the path soon faded to untracked tundra carpet. Her feet and flashlight led her confidently up, preventing her from veering too far right to cliff edges dropping to invisible, jagged spires on the south side of Mount Chapin.

After their daughter left on her solitary adventure, the parents continued to drive one-way Fall River Road up to Fall River Pass. Their headlights revealed more scenery than did their daughter's flashlight, but not much more. Two stone buildings were dim shadows as they drove across a mostly empty parking lot to a left turn onto Trail Ridge Road. Winding past its 12,120-foot highpoint, they circled back to the base of Fall River Road at the Lawn Lake Trailhead. Shouldering packs, the pair zigzagged up the Lawn Lake Trail toward a reserved campsite where they would spend the night to meet their daughter in the Roaring River drainage and welcome her back.

It was to be an admirable family tableau, but it did not happen. Bundled trailside in sleeping bags, they waited through an increasingly troubling night for a flashlight glow that never came bobbing through the gloom. At daybreak, they hurried back down the trail to report their daughter missing in the mountains.

Their report rang to the district ranger's desk at the Bighorn Ranger Station. It was not his preferred way to start the day. He deemed the call to be urgent for several reasons. Primarily, the girl was alone. His toughest ranger could trip into a tumble against a head-bashing rock. The terrain she challenged was packed with such rocks and many analogous hazards.

Moreover, the district ranger had to question if the gear she carried for a fast day hike would be adequate to keep her warm, fed, and dry through a cold night. Nights always were cold at her altitude. The previous evening, she had faced lightning, gusty wind, rain, and snow.

And how well did she really know these mountains that were dramatically distinguishable from her normal viewpoint on the east? Their appearance from her route on the west, uncarved by ancient glaciers, caused all the mountains she intended to traverse to appear confusingly similar.

The district ranger assembled an office team to direct search teams in the field to carry out the rescue. Searchers hiked the Lawn Lake Trail, some retracing the parents' hike of the previous day. Other searchers in the Roaring River drainage branched left toward Ypsilon Lake at the base of Ypsilon Mountain, a high point on her planned route. Descent into this area would have been a particularly dangerous route for the teen to have taken. Millennia of glacial-carving had not left gentle slopes on the east face of Ypsilon Mountain.

Another team followed the teen's intended route to Chapin Pass and then across open tundra to the summit of Ypsilon. This was the hopeful team, searching for the most likely happy rescue. Yet another team hiked beyond Ypsilon along the most treacherous part of her route, between Ypsilon and Fairchild Mountain. A USDA Forest Service helicopter hovered over all, searching three times and depositing search teams in their designated locations. Altogether, forty-five searchers strove in vain for a rescue the first day after the report of the missing mountaineer. Pizza and coffee sustained rescue planners through the night.

After the girl's second night in the cold, wet peaks, the park's chief ranger and Bighorn District ranger were directing rangers out searching, search dogs, a helicopter pilot and observer, and rangers commanding from the park headquarters. The total number of searchers grew to seventy-five.

Counting vice president of the United States Al Gore, the personnel involved grew to seventy-six.

The missing hiker's worried parents, with little else open to them amid the bustle of searchers, called their friend, the former senator from their home state, to see if he could offer any help from the White House. Thereafter, the park's dispatch operator directed a call from the White House operator to the chief ranger.

At the time, the chief ranger was learning that the helicopter was grounded by weather. He was telling all his searchers to remain in the field all through the coming night, if necessary, to find the missing teen. He was juggling advice and offers of help from palm readers, clairvoyants, and others blessed with sixth sense, and was shielding his subordinates from well-meaning folks with premonitions so that search and rescue operations could proceed unimpeded.

He suspected that all this pressure had inspired someone to relieve the tension with a joke. His immediate suspect was his Bighorn District ranger, who bore the most pressure, was near a phone, and was the nearest target for accusation. But, if a supposed call from the White House was waiting, the chief ranger had to take time to answer. He soon learned that Vice President Gore was, in fact, calling to learn if he could assist and to offer great encouragement.

A few minutes later, the chief ranger walked down the hall to the Bighorn District ranger's office to briefly distract him from the search and rescue with news of a call from the White House. It then was the district ranger's turn to accuse joking and to wish that making such a joke had occurred to him. Once the remarkable truth of the matter had been established, the two leaders had to decide whether or not to inform other team leaders about the interest of the vice president. They decided that their searchers would function better without this bit of information.

They could not tell Vice President Gore that all was well because it was not. They still could not find the teen.

Then the weather permitted the helicopter to fly, and its spotter saw bright items of clothing spread at tree line near Desolation Peaks, a short way outside the original search area. Hail and rain had driven the hiker from the high Mummy Range into the Hague Creek drainage.

Her training had taught her that hikers who are lost should stay in one place and wait to be found. She found what shelter she could amid trees and proceeded to pierce the mountain air with sharp blasts from the whistle she had placed in her pack for just such an eventuality. The helicopter and whistle combined to direct searchers on the ground to her. Her pack also had contained enough food and gear to support her through two cold, lonely, wet nights.

Doubtless, her parents were thankful that they and her camp had trained the girl well, that the search teams had exerted all possible effort to rescue her, and that the vice president of the United States, a prominent supporter of environmental causes, had directed the White House operator to call Rocky Mountain National Park.

FATAL FALL

Canyon Catastrophe

A s early as 1897, a visitor looked into the Grand Canyon of the Yellowstone and speculated that the precipitous walls were so high that the family of someone who fell over the edge would forget about their loved one before he hit the canyon floor. Even describing a landscape particularly suited to inspire competitive exaggeration, this statement was extreme. The canyon depth varies from 800 to 1,200 feet along its twenty-three-mile length.

For most people arriving at the canyon edge, this depth is adequate to inspire enough protective fear to prevent a fatal plunge. There are, however, relatively rare visitors who lack caution. When they fall, the rangers' resulting search and rescue duties make Yellowstone a temporarily unpleasant place in which to work.

Predictably, the majority of such tragedies occur in summer, when the park attracts most of its more than three million visitors to the crumbly canyon edge. The yellow-tinged stone that gives the park its name is rhyolite. It is relatively soft and easily eroded because it has been leached and decomposed by hot water over a geologically short ten to fourteen thousand years. Its (sometimes fatally) attractive Upper and Lower Falls drop over barriers of volcanic rhyolite that still resist the river's erosion. The cross-section shape of the canyon is an easy-to-see V because the rock is not strong enough to support absolutely vertical walls, such as seen in glacier-carved canyons typical of the sturdier rock in Grand Teton or Rocky Mountain National Parks. The V shape guarantees that falling bodies will crash into the walls before tumbling to the canyon floor.

The Lower Falls crash into the Grand Canyon of the Yellowstone.

The heat-degraded rock weathers easily into clay and sand, which function like ball bearings constantly replaced by nature on canyon edges, especially along approaches to viewpoints. The National Park Service has lined many of the popular approaches with barriers that do not prevent skinned hands and knees but generally do prevail against fatal tumbles due to grandeur-inspired inattention.

Of course, it would be physically impossible for NPS to build barriers to shield all cliffy places. Such Herculean construction would prevent all falls because it would make the canyon ugly enough to discourage most park visitors from traveling to view its colorful cliffs and oddly shaped hoodoos. Only bird watchers would crowd the cliffs to view osprey nests atop the hoodoos and watch parent birds deliver to their offspring fish snatched from the Yellowstone River.

Impressive as these wildlife and geological wonders are for summer visitors, the Grand Canyon of the Yellowstone may be even grander in winter, when it is seen only by the comparatively few visitors arriving by snowmobiles or on cross-country skis. The yellow, brown, and golden walls are accented by white snow. More visible in contrast to the very cold air are wisps of steam rising from hot springs at the canyon bottom. Their sulfurous fumes have altered iron minerals to splash the canyon with its famous colors.

Snow, of course, covers not only canyon ledges but also the path from the rim down to an overlook at the brink of the Lower Falls' 302-foot plunge into a hazy meeting between volcanically heated water and icy air. Several feet of Yellowstone's winter snow blanket the trail, covering summer's slippery gravel. The snow also provides its own brand of slickness and effectively lowers the barriers that protect summer visitors from gravity.

In February 1990 a father left his wife and two sons to enjoy the spectacle while he drove one of their snowmobiles to Fishing Bridge, deep within the park, where fuel was available. The understandably excited eleven- and twelve-year-old boys pushed ahead of their mother, at times three switchbacks beyond her, out of control on the rutted trail pocked by deep footprints left by previous visitors. The eleven-year-old slipped and fell on the trail, but snow protected him from the rough gravel. At the overlook, he slipped again and shot over the barrier to fall hundreds of feet to the massive ice cone that formed around the falls.

The next day, a search and rescue ranger swung in winter wind within the canyon confines at the end of a rope attached to a rented helicopter. It was a risky recovery of the boy's body.

The dead boy's parents sued the National Park Service for $10 million, maintaining that NPS was negligent for not posting a warning sign where the trail to the falls overlook began its descent. In July 1993 a US District Court judge denied their compensation claim for three reasons. First, federal law immunized from suit those decisions made by park employees acting in their "discretionary function." Second, the accident occurred within Wyoming, where state law stated that no claim could be sustained for injuries on land entered for recreational purposes if no fee was charged for that entry. NPS did not charge an entrance fee to Yellowstone for anyone under age sixteen.

Finally, the judge went beyond simply granting the federal government immunity. He criticized the boy's mother for letting her sons run 467 feet ahead, sometimes out of her sight, contrary to common sense on a trail she knew from her experience on it the previous summer was steep, with a sharp drop from the observation decks. He deemed the danger from snow on a steep surface to be obvious and held that "courts have universally required visitors to Yellowstone to exercise common sense when dealing with natural conditions."

Black Day in Black Canyon

———

In the state of Colorado, it is legal for a so-inclined individual to be drunk on alcohol and high on marijuana if not driving a motor vehicle. The state government does not bar folks who have diminished their mental acuity by ingesting mind-altering substances from wandering in the vicinity of high cliffs, very high cliffs. Use of marijuana, is banned in federally administered national parks despite state law, which holds a significant share of Colorado's high cliffs.

The highest cliff in the state is the Painted Wall in Black Canyon of the Gunnison National Park near Montrose. It is not really painted but is laced with interesting light-colored lines of igneous rock called pegmatite, frequently seen jazzing up the appearance of ubiquitous granite in the Rockies. The Painted Wall drops 2,250 very sudden feet. Unsurprisingly, such challenging but solid cliffs attract rock climbers like bees to honey, like ants to a picnic, like flies to . . . and so forth.

The Gunnison River began cutting this canyon through relatively recent and relatively soft volcanic rocks that have now eroded away. But before the volcanics departed, they trapped the Gunnison in a course that sliced down to extremely hard and old metamorphic and igneous rock. Confined to a channel that it would have swirled around if not trapped, the river kept flowing, but over rock so hard that less than a hair's thickness could be removed each year. Nonetheless, a million years here, a million there, added up to a seriously large amount of erosion and a very narrow canyon (forty feet wide at the river's narrowest channel), creating its gloomy grandeur. There are places between the canyon's very high and very close-set walls that on some days receive only thirty-three minutes of direct sunlight.

*The Painted Wall laced with light
igneous rock bands rises 2,250 feet
above the Black Canyon of the
Gunnison River and is the highest cliff
in Colorado.*

Historically, the lack of light has discouraged human penetration of the Black Canyon. Today's rock climbers, however, would design heaven to look like the Black Canyon of the Gunnison. The top of Black Canyon climbs are easier to reach via roads on gentler terrain than are the bases of the cliffs. The three trails leading from the top to below the South Rim are not only steep but also rough and unmaintained. The trail from Tomichi Point is the steepest.

Hiking and climbing in this very vertical park leads to injuries. Whether due to a turned ankle from a loose rock or a fall from a high point, some visitors need to be sought and rescued by the National Park Service and several volunteer rescue groups. These rescue preparations are in place although nearly all the injured begin their adventures completely sober with no reduced brain power.

NPS has a system to prevent visitors from undertaking recreation for which they are not fit. Everyone is banned from climbing particular cliffs during the time when peregrine falcons are nesting (mid-March until mid-summer). Otherwise, there is no banning of climbers or hikers, though they do have to obtain free wilderness use permits. Dispensing these permits gives rangers the opportunity to reasonably guess which park visitors might be injuries-about-to-happen and at least provide advice while noting where search and rescue teams might need to look first.

When a twenty-three-year-old University of Colorado student arrived at park headquarters for a wilderness use permit in June 2016, he triggered no concerns in the ranger issuing the permit. The permit was for the following day, which is common for park visitors intending an early start to reduce exposure to heat. Along with the permit came an explanation of what challenges could be involved.

The day before his hike, the student gave no indication to rangers that his proposed descent on June 9 and emergence on June 11 posed any extraordinary danger. He intended to get in touch with his family when he finished his hike. Late on June 11, the family called the park when they did not hear from him.

Early the next morning, rangers on foot began searching his proposed route, but they could not find him. The next day, they requested rental of a helicopter and spotted his body later that day at the base of a four-hundred-foot cliff, where they could not recover the corpse by foot. They achieved a recovery on June 14.

The student had been hiking by himself, a practice which NPS discourages but does not forbid. With slight cellphone coverage and a rugged landscape, a hiking partner might have been a lifesaver had the fall been incapacitating rather than instantly fatal.

Autopsy of such accident victims is typical to make sure they were not murdered and thrown off a cliff to disguise the crime. The autopsy of the Black Canyon victim indicated that his blood alcohol content was 0.211, more than twice the level that can lead to a drunk driving arrest. Moreover, his blood registered about double the amount of chemical (THC) that indicates driving under the influence of marijuana. Given that it is unremarkable for wilderness travelers in Black Canyon to require rescue when in full possession of their mental faculties, park rangers were dismayed that anyone would attempt to encounter the canyon while drunk or stoned.

However, a subsequent analysis of the normal decomposition of a body in a hot area (the Black Canyon in June tops eighty to ninety degrees) might indicate alcohol in a corpse that was not actually present prior to death. Because it took five hot days to recover the body, the chemical effects of decomposition might have explained the victim's blood alcohol level.

On the other hand, decomposition does not cause high marijuana blood levels. Because users do not expel marijuana chemicals naturally from their bodies until days after consumption, its use can cause fatal accidents and call for danger to search and rescue teams for unpredicted lengths of time.

Most visitors to the Black Canyon of the Gunnison, whether climbing its cliffs or driving its roads, believe that its wonder needs no chemical enhancement. Search and rescue teams believe this with particular passion.

Ranger Missing

A seasonal backcountry ranger got a ride up Old Fall River Road in late July 2005. A friend and fellow ranger in Colorado's Rocky Mountain National Park dropped off the patrol ranger at the Chapin Pass Trailhead to begin a tour along the Mummy Range. It was intended to be a one-day trip, circling down to the Lawn Lake Trailhead at the beginning of Old Fall River Road. Pickup was scheduled for 5:30 p.m.

However, the hike did not begin until 11:00 a.m. The time the patrol ranger allowed to complete his journey was wildly optimistic. For the ranger, this would be his first patrol across this terrain.

The intended route was up "C, C, and Y," Mounts Chapin and Chiquita and Ypsilon Mountain, the last two more than thirteen thousand feet above sea level. From Ypsilon, he expected to traverse a narrow ridge to the summit of Fairchild Mountain, another thirteener, then down to the rather oddly named "The Saddle" (not essentially different from uncounted other saddles between peaks in the national park). From the Saddle, a somewhat steep descent of alpine tundra would hit a trail down to Lawn Lake, then out to the trailhead in Horseshoe Park. It was a strenuous trip but not especially risky, except for typical summer lightning danger in long hours spent above tree line, which was fortunately absent that day.

The key factor would be long hours, just how long the ranger evidently did not realize, on mountains that he had not climbed previously. A projected completion time of six and a half hours was unreasonable even for a hiker possessing the ranger's excellent condition and stamina. He did not arrive at the trailhead to meet his ride home.

Viewed from the top of Mount Chiquita, the descent to the Roaring River drainage is more deadly than it looks.

Reasonable guesswork by hikers experienced with his planned route would speculate that he realized his scheduling error once above tree line. He might have skipped the steep ascent of tundra slopes to Mount Chapin on his way to the summit of Chiquita. Likely, he arrived at the low point between Chiquita and Ypsilon in full realization that he already was behind schedule and that the full route could not be completed in the time allotted.

A reasonable alternative might have seemed to find a shortcut east, down broad, comparatively unprecipitous terrain to meet the Ypsilon Lake Trail, more than two thousand feet below. He did not use his radio to contact park headquarters about his contemplated change in plans. This descent was technically less difficult than any other alternative route to meet his transportation rendezvous at the Lawn Lake Trailhead at the appointed time. But even the least challenging slope of the east face of the Mummy Range offers opportunities for a trip, tumble, and sudden stop against deadly rocks.

When the ranger failed to meet his ride at the Lawn Lake Trailhead, his friends began a mild search at his residence, at other trailheads, and at other non-backcountry locations. He might have been late, they thought, due to something he discovered on patrol. Finding something amiss, after all, was why he was walking a backcountry patrol.

The next day, search teams headed out to look for the missing ranger. Experienced search and rescue veterans were becoming highly concerned. By the second day of his disappearance, the search expanded drastically. Finally, a hundred searchers, dog teams, and five helicopters were seeking one of their own. They did not find him.

Nine days after his disappearance, three hikers who had not been part of the search effort came across the ranger's much-battered body. His injuries from a fall, though extensive, might have seemed at the time they occurred to be superficial though painful. He knew that head wounds were prone to heavy bleeding that made them seem worse than they were. He got a T-shirt from his pack and wrapped it around his head to staunch the bleeding. Then he limped along what seemed like the way out.

However, his head injuries were worse than he may have thought. He had suffered a fracture that caused bleeding inside his skull, which put sufficient pressure on his brain to kill him. After walking an unknowable distance, he passed out and died.

After the hikers happened on his body, guessing if the injury had been inevitably fatal was uncertain. Helicopter evacuation to the hospital in Estes Park Village might have saved him. But though his radio was in working order after the fall, he never called for help.

Why not? Clearly, he did not realize the seriousness of his injury. After all, he still could walk, until he could not, by which time he was likely unconscious. A clue to the injured ranger's motives might come from another, far less drastic fall suffered by an NPS ranger/naturalist.

Chasm Lake below the East Face of Longs Peak is arguably the most spectacular lake in the national park. Off-duty and out of uniform, a ranger/naturalist hiked there with family members to be present on the lakeshore early enough to watch alpenglow creep down the sheer face of the peak. Standing on a moderately large rock dropped by glaciers perhaps a thousand years previously, the naturalist was shoved by an unusual gust of severe wind into a stumble from the rock. The resulting face plant might have been recorded by earthquake monitors at the Colorado School of Mines in Golden.

The resulting dental damage and facial wounds were painful but not immobilizing. Worse for the naturalist was the embarrassment of having fallen. The naturalist, holding a scarf to cover the injury, could walk out but hid off the trail whenever a patrolling ranger came into view, easily spotted across treeless tundra. Dense lodgepole pine forest offered cover when other hikers were heard ascending the Longs Peak Trail below tree line.

In truth, a patrolling ranger likely could have done nothing to tend to the naturalist's injuries, which required a dentist and a physician. But the naturalist was embarrassed to be injured in a place that accounts for a distressing percentage of the search and rescue missions in Rocky Mountain National Park.

The naturalist had done nothing that would be deemed risky. Through bad luck, serious injury could happen in a trailhead parking lot. But a ranger/naturalist should be a source of aid rather than needing aid—or so it seemed. And unreasonable shame resulted.

Might the ranger who fell while descending from Chiquita have been too embarrassed to radio his fellows for rescue?

He had given himself too little time to patrol terrain he had not covered previously. He changed his route without radioing this change to headquarters; therefore, no one knew where to look for him when an accident happened. Many searchers risked injury themselves seeking him on dangerous slopes. And many people grieved and suffered from the death of a valuable contributor to society and a really nice guy.

RESCUERS

Jenny Lake Climbing Rangers

Falls by climbers unprotected by ropes are a common cause of death in Grand Teton National Park. The falling toll would be greater if not for the efforts of the Jenny Lake Climbing Rangers.

This team of about six permanent and fifteen seasonal rangers is long on experience. Some undertake this frequently dangerous search and rescue line of work for decades. The seasonals spend non-summer months teaching, freelance writing, instructing physical therapy, or guiding skiers. Search and rescue missions account for only 10 percent of their work in summer.

Much of the rest of their Teton jobs they call "preventative search and rescue," educating climbers and hikers about current backcountry conditions and climbing routes. Other ranger duties might include coordinating a search for a missing child, removing an unconscious motorist from a wrecked car, or venturing into the Snake River to retrieve a stranded boater. Despite their skill and heroism, they could make more money landscaping in the nearby town of Jackson, Wyoming. Nonetheless, the Jenny Lake Climbing Rangers tend to feel fortunate that they get paid to climb, their favorite activity in a pointy landscape that seems close to heaven.

The dramatic outline of the Teton Range has long lured climbers, likely before a claimed first ascent to the summit of Grand Teton by federal explorers in 1872. Other claimed firsts on the range's tallest peak were in 1893 and a certain ascent in 1899. For almost that long, other climbers have set out to rescue or recover their companions who met with bad luck (or had bad judgment).

Weathered limber pine frames the terrain overseen by the Jenny Lake Climbing Rangers.

Many seasonal rangers in the National Park Service work in various national parks over the years; the lure of working in different parks is clear. But the Jenny Lake seasonal rangers tend to return to the Tetons year after year, developing an esprit de corps. They need strong comradeship to constantly trust each other with their lives in the course of backcountry rescues. The climbing rangers can look at their comrades and know that they will always be ready to protect each other. It is a bond beyond what they find in most other work groups, a bond that's a necessity.

When the call for help comes, the search and rescue coordinator calls a team together at the Jenny Lake rescue building. All team members contribute their perspectives without hierarchy to assess the problem and plan the rescue. There is no ego, and each team member has an equal say as the team decides what needs to be done to achieve a successful result. They recognize the necessity that they approach each rescue with modesty. Frequent reminders in their work of their own mortality tend to control counterproductive confidence.

The team has been building group experience since its formation in 1952. Their assemblage, or cache, of rescue equipment is stored in a cabin at Jenny Lake dating from 1925, before the national park's establishment. In 1990 their ranger station, where rangers also issue climbing permits (permits may be discouraged, but not denied), was added to the National Register of Historic Places.

The Grand Teton alone attracts some four thousand climbers a year. Approximately half make it to the top. The climbing rangers try to match climbing routes with the experience of the climbers to reduce "10-100" radio calls signifying the need to recover a body.

However, each of the peaks in the Teton Range holds a set of risks. The first use of a helicopter in what has come to be called a "short-haul" technique took place in 1986 on Skillet Glacier, prominent on Mount Moran. It prevented a woman from dying of hypothermia in fading light. The technique involves a ranger descending a rope perhaps two hundred feet from a helicopter fighting to maintain stability while hovering in thin, high-altitude air not ideal for maintaining lift. At cliffy accident sites a helicopter has no room to land.

After first aid, the injured climber can be lifted into the sky at rope's end in either a body-enclosing sling or a stretcher. For those incapacitated but not otherwise injured, it can be the most thrilling experience the Tetons offer. The rangers consider short-haul to be the most dangerous of their duties. They practice often in preparation for using it as a very valuable rescue technique that has saved many lives (that otherwise would have been lost) by getting victims to a hospital in time.

Helicopters in particular and search and rescue operations in general cost substantial amounts of money in Grand Teton National Park, which concentrates much risk amid much dramatic scenery. Accident victims who are rescued never receive a bill. But a significant indication of the high regard held for the Jenny Lake Climbing Rangers is that a nonprofit organization has been formed to help fund their heroism through donations.

Search and Rescue Dogs

―――――――――

In 1994 a depressed young woman drove her car from the plains up a canyon into Rocky Mountain National Park. She parked her car near the Big Thompson River and disappeared.

A police bloodhound famous in Colorado for its tracking skills was brought in to search for the missing woman. At the parked car, the dog was presented with an article of the woman's clothing (a scent object) protruding from a plastic bag to protect its odor from irrelevant smells. "Search," his handler commanded. The bloodhound sniffed and at once took off running at the end of a twenty-foot-long leash, pulling his handler and chased by searchers running to keep up.

Down the unpaved road the dog proceeded until he encountered pavement. He followed the paved road through a broad meadow, then cut left when the road climbed over a forested ridge and down the other side to another broad meadow. Where the road met a highway, the bloodhound cut right, ears and jowls flapping and flying. He surged past the park entrance booths and then past the park headquarters. Onward he ran to a complicated intersection with roads branching in three directions. Not stopping for the traffic light, he raced undeterred by other human scents in the village of Estes Park. Pursuing rescuers strung out along the dog's path in exhaustion.

The humans began to think something was not right. The missing woman surely had not walked away from her car clear down to town.

No, she had not. Amazingly, impressively, remarkably, but not helpfully, the bloodhound followed her scent laid down hours previously when she had driven into the national park. A discouraging day was wasted. For dog

A bloodhound's keen sense of smell can be invaluable to police departments.

owners frustrated by the very many trials of search and rescue, it is encouraging to learn that following a trail in reverse is an error that can happen to even the best tracking dog.

The next day, the woman's family borrowed a neighbor's Australian shepherd, a breed whose forte is herding sheep rather than tracking. The National Park Service gave permission to take the dog where canines normally are banned, up the trail nearest the woman's parked car. The Australian shepherd led them to the woman's body at the base of a huge boulder carried to the spot by a glacier ten thousand years previously.

Bloodhounds can distinguish and follow a human scent originating from the approximately forty thousand skin cells each person drops every minute that are dispersed by air currents. (How many skin cells can escape from a moving car?) Most canines are wonderfully adept sniffers, though not as skillful as bloodhounds.

Although by far the best equipped for olfactory performance, blood-hounds are like many other exquisitely tuned instruments, unfortunately delicate. The world's best trackers tend to be subject to physical problems that make them relatively short-lived. This trait not only is heartbreak-ing for bloodhound trainers and handlers, but also makes the best canine trackers rare and expensive.

Although not as wondrous as bloodhounds, various other breeds can be good enough for search and rescue work. Doubtless, many Chihuahua owners have witnessed their dogs exhibiting excellent smelling ability. But search and rescue dogs also need to be sturdy enough to traverse rough, often dangerous, ground for hours in all kinds of weather. Their handlers, of course, face the same conditions.

Search and rescue dogs frequently work in bright orange harnesses to help handlers keep their partners in sight in thick brush or dim light. The vests also notify located victims (who inevitably see the dogs before they see the human team members) that the dogs are helpers come to rescue. And their search and rescue attire also reminds the dogs that they are on a mission rather than a romp.

In addition to a scent object, the handler carries a strip of cloth with which to keep track of wind direction. Following the handler, a second human, map in hand, guarantees that the search team stays on course and skips no terrain. A team radio keeps the searchers in contact with other teams and with leaders directing the search.

The most common breeds for this work include Labrador retrievers, German shepherds, golden retrievers, Belgian herding breeds, and some-what smaller border collies. If they came equipped with thumbs, border collies likely could learn to type after-search reports.

Rescue dog training best begins with puppies as young as twelve weeks. As they reach a year old, basic obedience classes in sit, stay, down, come, and heel can make training for search and rescue less difficult.

Note *less difficult*, rather than easier. This training never is any degree of easy. It can be monotonous for dogs and trainers, and many dogs and handlers fail. Starting with an adult dog makes training harder, but not impossible.

Training almost always is accomplished through the aid of a group of likeminded and motivated owners. The training itself is a more-than-one-person job. Mutual psychological support makes the effort fun.

Most canine search and rescue is carried out by volunteers who must spend a significant amount of time and money. The need for search and rescue dogs never comes at convenient times. The phone rings at midnight, and gear for dog and handler needs to be already in the car. The handler fumbles into field attire. The dog, in a considerably better mood, jumps into the crate in the car, which acts as a canine safety belt. It may be a drive of a few hours to the search site, or it may be a drive to the nearest airport. It is not cheap, and it is not a party.

Because canine search and rescue teams are essential to many types of police and first responder work, it is fortunate that many owners stand ready to volunteer and train with their dogs for this duty. Why do they tolerate hours of training several days a week, the expense of gas and travel, hard physical work demanding agility of human and dog where someone already has gotten into trouble, and, perhaps most trying, plunging dog and handler into emotional trauma?

They do it because few things can instill so much warm joy as teaming with a dog to save a life.

ABOUT THE AUTHOR

KENT DANNEN has been told that writing a book is easy: "Just stare at a computer screen until little drops of blood pop out on your forehead." But he did not have to sweat blood to research and recount stories about search and rescue labor and courage in the Rocky Mountains. His editor told him to have fun; he did.

Kent's previous books, such as *Hiking Rocky Mountain National Park,* 10th edition, and *Best Hikes Colorado's Indian Peaks Wilderness*, required walking, walking, walking through joyful, spectacular wilderness. Researching search and rescue stories required driving, reading, and staring at maps and photos from the Canadian border to northern New Mexico. It all was uplifting.

Inspired by the view from his home near Allenspark, Colorado, and informed by memories and notes from national parks, historic sites, libraries, and museums, Kent created less wear on his boots than on other items of apparel. He dreamed of heroes (mostly) and their glories. He never sweated blood.

Kent Dannen and Ch. Runner keep warm in January on the South Rim of the Grand Canyon.